Living without Religion

OTHER BOOKS BY PAUL KURTZ

LIVING WITHOUT RELIGION

Eupraxsophy

Paul Kurtz

 Prometheus Books

59 John Glenn Drive
Amherst, New York 14228-2197

This book is a reprint of *Eupraxophy: Living without Religion* (1989). The work has also been published in Germany as *Leben Ohne Religion: Eupraxophie.*

Published 1994 by Prometheus Books

Inquiries should be addressed to
Prometheus Books, 59 John Glenn Drive, Amherst, New York 14228–2197.
VOICE: 716–691–0133, ext. 207.
FAX: 716–564–2711.
WWW.PROMETHEUSBOOKS.COM

Library of Congress Card Catalog N. 88–64167
ISBN 0–87975–929–1

Printed in the United States of America on acid-free paper

Contents

5

Acknowledgments

I am pleased to thank the many people who read or discussed the manuscript of this book with me and offered valuable suggestions: Joe Barnhart, Paul Beattie, Vern Bullough, Fred Condo, Doris Doyle, Cynthia Dwyer, Beverly Earles, Joseph Fletcher, Thomas Flynn, Thomas Franczyk, Sidney Hook, Gerald Larue, Timothy Madigan, Molleen Matsumura, Delos McKown, Irvin Leibowitz, Verle Muhrer, Patricia Pederson-Lawton, Howard Radest, Ranjit Sandhu, Andrée Spuhler, Harry Stopes-Roe, Rob Tielman, Thomas Vernon, and Robert Worsfold.

I. What Is Eupraxsophy?

IS HUMANISM A RELIGION?

The question "What is humanism?" is often asked today, as the term is used with greater frequency. Many authors, including some prominent humanists, have called humanism a religion, maintaining that humanism will in time transform the ancient religious systems and eventually supplant them. Julian Huxley predicted that humanistic religion would become a new "religion without revelation."[1] John Dewey distinguished the *religious* from *religion* and said that the religious qualities of experience could more appropriately be fulfilled in the contemporary world through a new naturalistic humanism that expressed our ideal values and our commitment to science and democracy.[2] Dewey used a naturalized conception of "God." His concept did not denote a transcendent being but simply expressed the union of our ideal ends. Religion to him therefore functioned primarily in ethical terms as a form of conduct.

Humanism construed in this way bears many similarities to traditional systems of religious belief. Christianity, Judaism, Hinduism, Islam, and Buddhism; for they each set forth a way of life. Paul Tillich, the existential Protestant theologian, defined

9

religion as that which expresses our "ultimate concern"—whether it be the morality of Jesus or Buddha, or of a sophisticated, postmodern scientific secularist.[3] In this sense, humanism is said to perform psychological, sociological, and existential functions similar to those of theistic systems of belief. Interestingly, most major humanist organizations in North America have followed the religious model, attempting to create societies, chapters, or churches that would perform the functions of traditional religions—albeit without their content.

I think that this interpretation of humanism is profoundly flawed, for it glosses over important differences between theism and humanism. The term *secular* humanism has thus been introduced to distinguish it from *religious* humanism. Sidney Hook, Joseph Fletcher, Corliss Lamont, and other leading humanists maintain that humanism is a secular philosophical, scientific, and ethical outlook.[4] They deny that it has certain of the essential characteristics of a religion. In particular, humanism does not assert a god or other sacred realities, nor does it carry with it the distinctive symbols or functions of traditional religions. Many of the precursors of contemporary humanism—Marx, Nietzsche, Freud, Sartre, Russell—have been strong critics of theistic religion, which they considered to be divisive and illusionary; they suggested new directions, following reason, for humankind to take.[5]

Is it possible to lead an authentic life without religiosity? Or are there some functions inherent in the human condition that only a religious system of beliefs and practices can fulfill? Humanists deplore the fact that orthodox religious systems persist in spite of massive critiques leveled against them over the ages by skeptical philosophers and scientists. They are dismayed that when old religious forms are abandoned, new cults of unreason often arise to take their place. Are humans by nature religious animals? Will not humanism as a guide to leading a good life continue to flounder until it begins to address these questions? In *The Transcendental Temptation: A Critique of Religion and the Para-*

normal,[6] I have dealt at length with these puzzles, pointing to a deep hunger for the transcendental within the human breast, manifesting itself throughout history in various religious forms. Religions are projections of wishful fantasies; the systems of belief and practices that persist apparently satisfy some deep-seated human needs. Can one substitute moral equivalents for traditional religions? Can these give meaning to life? Can they inspire men and women to fulfill their highest aspirations without any transcendental fixation? Can human beings lead responsible lives without a supernatural support for ethics? I answer: Yes. In *Forbidden Fruit: The Ethics of Humanism,*[7] I have outlined a thoroughly humanistic, ethical philosophy. I submit that there are common moral decencies (that is, general ethical principles governing social interactions) that are widely recognized and followed in human cultures. Moreover, it is possible for individuals to lead lives of excellence and to respect the rights of others without theistic pretensions or sanctions.

The question I wish to address in this book is whether it is possible to adopt an *areligious* or *nonreligious* approach to life and still find human life to be full of conviction and inspiration. Given the failure until now to build strong humanist institutions as alternatives to traditional religions, these questions are all the more compelling.

A new dimension has been added to this argument by the fact that many conservative theistic critics of humanism now accept the earlier claim of some humanists that humanism is a religion. This is paradoxical, because liberal religious humanists had previously argued, against the steadfast opposition of theists, that a belief system without God functioned religiously and was entitled to all the exemptions and privileges that theistic religions enjoyed.

Today we are confronted with a new challenge, for conservative theists not only say they agree with this claim but go further. Even *secular* humanism, they insist, is a "religion," and as such it must be bound by all the limits placed on theistic religions in democratic societies. This argument is particularly cutting in the American context, for the First Amendment to the United States Constitution explicitly forbids the establishment of a religion.[8] The critics of humanism maintain that there has been a de facto establishment of secular humanism in the modern world, especially in the public schools and the judicial system. If secular humanism is a religion, they insist, then it has no right to a privileged place; for example, it cannot be taught to the young, using public funds and in the guise of neutrality.[9]

No doubt this argument is limited in its scope to the current political and legal battles in the United States and will in time pass. But there is a more profound issue that is likely to have continuing theoretical and practical import—namely, does a scientific world view, a naturalistic ethical theory, or a democratic political ideology of necessity have "religious" significance and functions? And is this religious component essential to and inevitable in secular philosophies? Critics of secular humanism and modernism such as Richard Neuhaus deplore the fact that religion has been excluded from greater influence in open and modern democratic societies,[10] and they are determined to restore it to public life. In an extreme position, the critics of scientific humanism consider evolution to be only a theory, on a par with creationism, one that expresses the bias of "the religion of secular humanism." Are the cultivation of moral education and the development of critical intelligence in the young religious, as they claim? Are the study of the social sciences and the teaching of history—or indeed anything or everything that is Bible-neutral or that draws upon critical scholarship and science—to be considered "secular" or "humanistic," and hence "religious"?

Even more pointedly, we may ask whether Marxism is or has become a religion. Many consider Karl Marx to have been the leading secular thinker of the nineteenth century; he has surely been the most influential one. Who could have imagined in the late nineteenth century that Marx's theories would have been put into practice by Communist and Socialist parties in the twentieth century and that they would have such a massive impact on events? Marxists in power have destroyed many of the old institutions—including the power of *l'église ancienne*—which were often wedded to privileged economic interests. Have the state structures that Communist parties built been transformed into a new state church, performing many of the roles of traditional religion? Has Marxism thus been transformed into a religion?

Unsympathetic critics have pointed out the emergence of Marxist heroes to replace the saints, the growth of a new dogma and creed (the dialectic), and the need of a party bureaucracy to build institutions of control to supplant those of traditional churches. Marxist ideals seem to provide many with an inspiring faith, and a revolutionary fervor motivates the commissar-priest. This was especially true of Leninist, Stalinist, and Maoist versions of Marxism, but not of democratic socialist varieties, which explicitly renounced the cult of personality and totalitarian structures. There has been widespread disenchantment with the totalitarian and dogmatic versions of Marxism. Disillusionment and stagnation have overtaken the revolutionary fervor of earlier generations. Significant reforms are being undertaken in the Marxist world today, and it is difficult to predict what will eventually ensue.

We have been raising large questions, which depend in part upon the meaning of the term *religion*. Are Zen Buddhism and Confucianism religions? And if so, why not Epicureanism and Stoicism? After all, they are practical systems of belief that advocated an ethical outlook and way of life. And if these, why not humanism and Marxism? Can *religion* be stretched to encompass all of these systems, or should it be used in a more restricted sense? At one time I was persuaded to extend the term *religious* to incorporate a wide range of humanist beliefs and practices, for I noted the passionate commitment that humanism could arouse.[11] If nothing else, it seemed to me then to have been a wise strategy for the humanist movement to adopt, that is, to consider itself a religion of the future.[12]

I now think that this line of reasoning was and is fallacious. For if we argue in this way, then we must ask, "What is *not* a religion?" If anything that expresses our "Ultimate concern" is to be viewed as a religion, then might not this term also apply to libertarianism, socialism, atheism, feminism, vegetarianism; that is, to any movement that expresses someone's highest ideals and aspirations, gives direction and meaning, and provides a way of life?

If so, then virtually anything can be considered a religion, as long as it is taken passionately and seriously. Then why not science, history, chess, sports, sex, or any activity to which we pledge our deepest commitment? The Achilles heel of this argument is that it is theistic religions that have transformed themselves historically by assuming all-encompassing nonreligious moral, psychological, and sociological functions. The fact that religions may share these functions with other human interests and institutions does not make these other interests and institutions religious.

The point is that there are profound differences between a theistic approach to reality and morality on the one hand, and a scientific, naturalistic, and secular humanist approach on the other. The former claims that there is a "sacred" and "divine" character to reality, one to which they are supremely devoted. Humanists reject this basic assumption. Humanists believe that we need to summon our own resources and to develop critical intelligence to solve our problems. Accordingly, the key humanist virtue is courage, the courage to become, in spite of the sometimes tragic character of human existence. Humanism focuses on this life and the here and now; it does not project a supernatural realm of sacred mysteries underlying our transactions with nature. It does not have any expectations of salvation, nor is there any sense that we are duty-bound to revere the unknown.

In my judgment, unless the point is made that humanism is *not* a religion, humanism will continue to languish. I submit that a chief reason why a genuine humanism has thus far failed to have a greater impact on social institutions and to replace classical religion is that it has attempted to ape religion. The next stage for human progress is to overcome the transcendental temptation by building imaginative alternative institutions. But fast humanism must make a radical break with those forms of religious humanism that cloud this distinction. Humanism needs to affirm that human beings can lead authentic lives *without* religious pretensions. It needs to move *beyond* religion.

In making a distinction between a nonreligious, secular humanism and religious humanism, I surely do not wish to fracture the humanist movement. But there already exists a deep division on this point. Many religious humanists continue to insist not only that they are religious but that secular humanism is a religion. They especially look to humanistic Unitarian churches, Ethical Culture societies, or Humanistic Judaism temples as their models. Most Unitarian churches or societies are not humanist, but are vaguely Christian, or theistic, even though a significant number of Unitarians identify with humanism. Even in humanist churches, societies, and temples, there is a minister or leader who tends his congregation, delivers sermons on Sundays, and administers pastoral counseling—as do his theistic counterparts. Granted that the religious humanist is a nontheist who rejects the existence of God; yet in adopting the term *religious*, he only obfuscates the true character of humanism as a radical alternative to theism.

EUPRAXSOPHY DEFINED

If humanism is not a religion, what is it? Unfortunately, there is no word in the English language adequate to describe it fully—though there are words in other languages that do. Humanism combines, as I will argue, a method of inquiry, a cosmic world view, a life stance, and a set of social values. The Dutch, for example, have the word *levensbeschouwing*, which can be translated as "reflection on, consideration of, or view of life." Dutch also has the adjective *levensovertuiging*, which is stronger than *levensbeschouwing* because *overtuiging* means "conviction." Thus there are no religious overtones. *Religion* in Dutch is *godsdienst*, which means "service to God." English has no such terminology.

Accordingly, I think we will have to coin a new term in order to distinguish nontheistic beliefs and practices from other systems of beliefs and practices, a term that could be used in many languages. The best approach is to combine Greek roots. I have come up with the term *eupraxsophy*, which means "good practical wisdom." *Eupraxsophy* is derived from the following roots: *eu-*, *praxis*, and *sophia*. *Eu-* is a prefix which means "good," "well," "advantageous." It is combined in words such as *eudaeomonia*, which means "well-being" or "happiness"; it is also used in *euthanasia, eulogy, euphoria*, etc. *Praxis* (or *prassein*) refers to "action, doing, or practice." *Eupraxia* means "right action" or "good conduct." The suffix *sophia* is derived from *sophos* ("wise") and means "wisdom." This suffix appears in the term *philosophy*, combining *philos* ("loving") and *sophia* ("wisdom") to mean "love of wisdom."

In its original sense, philosophy, as metaphysics or "the science of being," investigated the general principles and categories by which we can understand nature and interpret reality. The classical philosophers attempted to work out a system of nature in which certain principles were considered to be basic. Metaphysics has been in considerable disrepute in modern times, particularly in the hands of skeptical critics. At the very least, metaphysics analyzes and interprets the basic concepts of the sciences, attempts to make some sense out of them, and, if possible, to unify them. This is a very complex task today because of the continuing proliferation of new fields of learning and the enormous difficulty of any one mind being able to master the expanding corpus of knowledge.

Philosophical inquiry also focuses on epistemology, the theory of knowledge. It is concerned with questions of meaning, truth, the principles of valid inference, inductive and deductive logic. There are many other branches of philosophy, including logic, aesthetics, ethics, the philosophy of science, political and social philosophy, and the philosophy of religion; indeed, almost any field can be approached philosophically.

Synthetic philosophy attempts to offer universal or general principles and to develop an overall view, a cosmic perspective or *Weltanshauung*. This is sometimes called synoptic or speculative philosophy, but since the development of modern science in the sixteenth and seventeenth centuries, this approach has been seriously questioned on methodological grounds, for it cannot be done independently of science but only in relation to it. Nonetheless, philosophy, in this sense, is thinking about generalities; it is concerned with root questions and cosmic coherence. Analytic and critical philosophy, on the other hand, are far more modest in scope. Analytic philosophy is concerned with understanding the nature of meaning and truth, and in defining and analyzing the key concepts within any particular field of inquiry. Critical philosophy is evaluative; it strives for clarity, but it also seeks to appraise the validity of truth claims.

These activities are primarily intellectual in purpose, and they are neutral in regard to their practical consequences. The Greeks distinguished contemplative from practical wisdom. Philosophy, as the love of wisdom, begins primarily in the theoretical or contemplative mode. There is another branch of normative philosophy, however, that strives for practical wisdom in ethics and politics. Here, classical philosophy sought to provide some guidance for the good life and the just society. Aristotle maintained in the *Nicomachean Ethics* that ethics has practical import and that we should study it in order to live well. He held that the development of character and virtue and the exercise of practical wisdom would contribute to the achievement of happiness. Many ethical philosophers, however, have focused primarily on the meta-analysis of concepts such as "good," "bad," "virtue," "value," "justice," etc. This was expanded in latter-day Kantian philosophy to the definitions of "right," "wrong," "obligation," "responsibility," etc. Whether or not these terms can be defined has been hotly debated down to the present;[13] objectivists believe that they can be defined, but there is a skeptical tradition which denies their definability. Be that as it may, classical ethics always had a normative purpose.

A basic distinction can be made between *customary morality*, which refers to the moral conceptions that already prevail in a given cultural group, and *ethics*, which involves a reflective and critical component. Today, many philosophers concerned with ethics emphasize the need for ethical rationality—but virtually for its own sake; and many eschew making any concrete recommendations beyond this in dealing with problems that arise in customary morality. This is particularly true in universities and colleges, where philosophy is taught as an academic discipline, where philosophers do philosophical research and publish their disquisitions in scholarly journals, and where philosophy teachers have no clearly identifiable positions. They consider their primary pedagogical method to be the presentation of alternative philosophical theories and do not attempt to inculcate a set of beliefs or values; that is, they do not seek to persuade their students or the general public to accept their philosophical outlook. Since their task is pure inquiry, similar to that of other disciplines, such as history and the natural and social sciences, they can safely retreat into splendid isolation in an ivory tower—philosophers *qua* philosophers—and do not have to vindicate their personal positions. The virtue of this form of philosophy is that the professor imparts a love of wisdom and the skills of critical thinking without imposing his or her own biases on the student. The professor does not wish to indoctrinate or propagandize for a particular cosmic outlook. He or she wants to be "objective"; he may even be fearful of reprisals from those who support the conventional wisdom of the day. Yet this kind of philosophy does not satisfy the deeper queries of students and ordinary men and women. It presents no world view; it does not defend a theory of meaning and truth; nor does it seek to persuade others of the comparative reasonableness of the philosopher's own considered normative or social ideology. Philosophy, as the love of wisdom, aside from being committed to fair-minded and objective critical analysis, must be *neutral*. It can take no position; it can draw no normative conclusions from its formal analyses. It is largely a cognitive enterprise; it involves no attitudinal or emotive component. Nor does it seek to arouse conviction or inspire commitment.

How far philosophy has come from the Socratic vision of the good life! For Socrates, philosophy had direct relevance to how we should live. The unexamined life is not worth living, he averred, and he was even willing to die for his convictions. Spinoza's *Ethics* seems to have expressed both a philosophy and a eupraxsophy, at least implicitly. We might even say that many or most philosophical systems implicitly had a pragmatic function and that their task was to provide an alternative to religion and a guide to ethics and politics. Contemplative wisdom was often a mask for deeper utilitarian purposes. Marx clearly marked a break with the contemplative mode of philosophy, particularly when he said that the task of philosophy was not simply to interpret the world but also to *change* it! Philosophy in this sense has momentous significance—as it did for Nietzsche, Schopenhauer, Russell, Sartre, Dewey, and others. Alas, today it has become wedded to the academy and corrupted by narrow specialization. Philosophy has lost out to religion and ideology, which in competition for the souls of men and women now rule the day. That is why we need to take new directions and to carve out a new approach.

Eupraxsophy differs from antiseptically neutral philosophy in that it enters consciously and forthrightly into the marketplace where ideas contend. Unlike pure philosophy, it is not simply the *love* of wisdom, though this is surely implied by it, but also the *practice* of wisdom. By that I do not mean that ethicists should not be interested in developing the capacity for critical ethical judgment or practical wisdom. That is an eminent goal. But eupraxsophy goes further than that, for it provides a coherent, ethical life stance. Moreover, it presents a cosmic theory of reality that seems reasonable at a particular point in history in the fight of the best knowledge of the day. Humanist eupraxsophy defends a set of criteria governing the testing of truth claims. It also advocates an ethical posture. And it is committed implicitly or explicitly to a set of political ideals. Eupraxsophy combines both a *Weltanshauung* and a philosophy of living. But it takes us one step further by means of commitment; based upon cognition, it is fused with passion. It involves the application of wisdom to the conduct of life.

Noneupraxic philosophies are unwilling to affirm this conviction. They examine all sides of a question, see the limits and pitfalls of each, but are unwilling to take a stand on any. As I have said, this has some merit; for the open mind must recognize that it may be mistaken and that views may have to be modified in the light of new arguments or evidence. Thus, one needs to be skeptical—but not at the price of forfeiting all convictions. The *eupraxsopher* does make a choice—the most reasonable one in light of the available evidence—and this enables him to act. After all, theologians, politicians, generals, engineers, businessmen, lawyers, doctors, artists, poets, and plain men and women have beliefs, and they act. Why deny this right to the informed philosopher-eupraxsopher? Surely, however, one's beliefs should be based upon reason, critical intelligence, and wisdom. This is what the suffix *sophy* refers to. Wisdom in the broad sense includes not only philosophical and practical judgment, but also scientific understanding.

Let us turn to *Webster's Dictionary* for a definition of *sophia* or *wisdom*:

> 1. The quality of being wise; ability to judge soundly and deal sagaciously with facts, especially as they relate to life and conduct; knowledge, with the capacity to make due use of it; perception of the best ends and the best means; discernment and judgment; discretion; sagacity. 2. Scientific or philosophical knowledge.

Explicit in this definition is a scientific component, for wisdom includes the best scientific knowledge drawn from research and scholarship in the various fields of inquiry. Unfortunately, the various scientific specialists often feel qualified to judge only matters within their own areas of competence, leaving out the broader questions that have a direct bearing on life. There is a crisis in modern science, for the specialties are growing exponentially, with many specialists feeling that they can talk only to those within their own disciplines. Science thus has become fragmented. Who is able to cross the boundary lines and draw meta-inferences about nature, the human species, society, or life in general? The eupraxsopher deems it his mission to do so.

Theoretical scientific research is morally neutral. The scientist is interested in developing causal hypotheses and theories that can be verified by the evidence. Scientists describe or explain how the subject under study behaves, without evaluating it normatively. There is, of course, a pragmatic element to science, particularly the applied sciences; for we constantly seek to apply our scientific know-how to practical technology. Moreover, the scientist presupposes epistemological criteria that govern his process of inquiry. He is committed to a set of values:

truth, clarity, consistency, rationality, objectivity. But the scientist *qua* scientist does not go beyond that, and he restricts himself in the quest for knowledge to his specialized domain of inquiry.

Humanist eupraxsophy, on the other hand, attempts to draw the philosophical implications of science to the life of man. It seeks to develop a cosmic perspective, based on the most reliable findings encountered on the frontiers of science. It recognizes the gaps in knowledge and the things we do not know that still need to be investigated. It is keenly aware of the need for fallibilism, and agnosticism about what we do and do not know. Yet it boldly applies practical scientific wisdom to life.

Eupraxsophy, unlike philosophy or science, does not focus on one specialized field of knowledge; it seeks to understand the total impact of scientific knowledge on a person's life. Yet the areas of philosophy, science, and eupraxsophy are not rigid. Philosophers can assist scientists in interpreting their discoveries and relating them to other fields of inquiry, and in developing a broader point of view. Still, eupraxsophy moves beyond philosophy and science in seeking to present a coherent life view as the basis on which we are willing to act. It is the ground upon which we stand, the ultimate outlook that controls our view of reality.

Accordingly, the primary task of eupraxsophy is to understand nature and life and to draw concrete normative prescriptions from this knowledge. Eupraxsophy thus draws deeply from the wells of philosophy, ethics, and science. It involves at least a double focus: a cosmic perspective and a set of normative ideals by which we may live.

NOTES

1. Julian Huxley, *Religion Without Revelation* (London: Watts, 1927).

2. John Dewey, *A Common Faith* (New Haven: Yale University Press, 1934).

3. Paul Tillich, *The Courage to Be* (New Haven: Yale University Press, 1952); *The Dynamics of Faith* (New York: Harper & Row, 1957); *Systematic Theology*, vols. 1–3 (Chicago: University of Chicago Press, 1951, 1963).

4. Sidney Hook, *The Quest for Being* (New York: St. Martin's Press, 1961); Joseph Fletcher, "Is Secular Humanism a Religion?" *Free Inquiry* 6, no. I (Winter 1985/1986); Corliss Lamont, *The Philosophy of Humanism* (New York: Friedrich Unger, 1965).

5. Karl Marx, *Economic and Philosophic Manuscripts of 1844*; Friedrich Wilhelm Nietzsche, *Thus Spake Zarathustra*; Sigmund Freud, *The Future of an Illusion and Moses and Monotheism*; Jean-Paul Sartre, *Being and Nothingness*; Bertrand Russell, *On God and Religion*, ed. by Al Seckel (Amherst, N.Y.: Prometheus Books, 1986).

6. Paul Kurtz, *The Transcendental Temptation: A Critique of Religion and the Paranormal* (Amherst, N.Y.: Prometheus Books, 1986).

7. Paul Kurtz, *Forbidden Fruit: The Ethics of Humanism* (Amherst, N.Y.: Prometheus Books, 1988).

8. The First Amendment reads: "Congress shall make no law respecting the establishment of religion or prohibiting the free exercise thereof."

9. This argument has been advanced by John W. Whitehead on legal grounds. See *The Second American Revolution* (Westchester, M.: Crossway Books, 1985). It was a decision in the Mobile, Alabama, case in 1987, when Judge Brevard Hand ruled that secular humanism was a religion; the Supreme Court later overturned his decision.

10. Richard J. Neuhaus, *The Naked Public Square: Religion and Democracy in America* (Grand Rapids, Mich.: Eerdmans, 1984).

11. Paul Kurtz, "Functionalism and the Justification of Religion," *Journal of Religion* 38, no. 3 (July 1958); *The Fullness of Life* (New York: Horizon Books, 1974).

12. See especially *Humanist Manifesto I* (1933), which considered humanism to be a religion. Reprinted in *Humanist Manifestos I and II*, ed. by Paul Kurtz (Amherst, N.Y.: Prometheus Books, 1973).

13. This is especially true in twentieth-century ethics, among such

philosophers as G. E. Moore (*Principia Ethica*, Cambridge, 1903), the deontologists W. D. Ross and H. A. Prichard, and the emotivists A. J. Ayer and C. L. Stevenson.

II. What Is Humanism?

Humanism is a eupraxsophy. But it is not unique; there have been other eupraxsophies historically. In the Greek and Roman world, Epicureanism, Stoicism, and skepticism were eupraxsophies. Each had a metaphysical world view, each made concrete ethical recommendations about how to achieve the good life, and each had epistemological theories. There have been many other kinds of eupraxsophies: utilitarianism, Marxism, existentialism, pragmatism, perhaps even Confucianism and some forms of Buddhism; each contain various elements of eupraxsophy. Some of these schools, however, are concerned primarily with *eupraxia* (that is, with good practice) and they deemphasize the *sophia*, the scientific and philosophic world view. Some, such as Marxism and utilitarianism, focus primarily on *social praxis*.

There are many variations of humanism: naturalistic, existential, Marxist, pragmatic, and liberal. We may ask, what is distinctive about the eupraxsophy of modern-day secular humanism? I wish to propose a definition of humanism that is thoroughly secular. This definition is not arbitrary, since it classifies a set of propositions held by many scientists and philosophers who consider themselves to be humanists. Nonetheless, it involves a prescriptive recommendation about how to use the term *humanism*. Humanism includes at least four main characteristics: (1) it is a method of inquiry; (2) it presents a cosmic world view; (3) it contains a concrete set of ethical recommendations for the individual's life stance; and (4) it expresses a number of social and political ideals.

A METHOD OF INQUIRY

An essential characteristic of contemporary secular humanism is its commitment to a method of inquiry. This feature is so important that it may even be said to function as the basic principle of secular humanism. Questions concerning meaning and truth have been enduring ones in the history of philosophy, and they have come to the forefront since the growth of modern science. Epistemology is also pivotal to secular humanism.

Humanist epistemology may be defined first by what it opposes. It rejects the use of arbitrary authority to obfuscate meaning or to legislate truth. Throughout human history there have been persistent attempts by institutional authorities to do precisely that. The church and the state have been especially prone to define, codify, and enforce orthodoxy. The need for social order is such that humankind finds it useful or necessary to regulate conduct. Custom ensures some stability in social behavior and enables human beings to function with a clear understanding of expectations and of the acceptable parameters of civilized discourse and conduct. The rules of the game by which we live and work together are established—in constitutions, bylaws, contracts, laws, and regulations—and they enable us to fulfill our cooperative aims. It is one thing, however, to lay down the rules of conduct by law and to enforce them by sanction, leaving opportunities for them to be modified and revised in democratic societies. It is quite another to uphold unchanging orthodoxy of belief in the sciences, philosophy, literature, the arts, politics, morality, or religion and to seek to legislate acceptable modes of personal behavior. Here the appeal to authority is illegitimate, for it substitutes a conformist faith for intelligently grounded knowledge. Establishing orthodoxy in belief stifles discovery and blocks inquiry. Transmitting the fixed beliefs of an early age to future ones prevents bold new departures in thought. Even the most cherished beliefs so lovingly defended in time may become archaic; blatant falsehoods persist as prejudice encrusted by habits.

History is replete with pathetic attempts by past civilizations to enshrine their belief systems in perpetuity. Efforts to censor conflicting opinions have often led to violent social conflict. In worst-case scenarios such suppression degenerates into sheer tyranny over the human mind. Dictators, ecclesiastical princes, and vested oligarchs have tried to police the thoughts of everyone under their jurisdiction, using the Holy Inquisition, the Gestapo, or the NKVD to suppress dissent. In a weaker form, conformist pressures substitute public opinion or that of the leading authorities of the day for creative and independent inquiry. Abiding by conventional wisdom thus stifles new ideas. No one group can claim to have a monopoly on wisdom or virtue, and to proclaim one's fondest convictions as *obiter dicta* for everyone in the society is destined to fail. Even though power is the chief criterion for the perpetuation of a belief system, that is no guarantee of social stability, for the so-called authorities often disagree about truth. The reigning beliefs of one age may become the intransigent follies of the next. Thoughtless bigots wish to prevent any questioning of their revered articles of faith; they are fearful of change and challenge. Regrettably, all of the major religious orthodoxies historically have succumbed to the temptation to enforce their beliefs—when and where they had the power to do so—and to impose their practices upon the rest of society. Orthodoxies have allowed fanatic intolerance to prevail, and they have denied the right of those who disagree to voice their contrary faiths or dissenting opinions.

The same narrow mindset appears in powerful political and economic elites, who fear any challenge to their privileged positions and thus seek to enforce by law what they consider to be the only legitimate system of belief. They strain to exclude outsiders who threaten their hegemony by declaring them political heretics or religious infidels.

In religion, orthodox belief systems are rooted in ancient dogmas held to be so sacred that they are immune to objective examination. The claims made in the name of God are shrouded in privileged revelations received from on high. The claims to divine authority are shielded from critical scrutiny by popes, cardinals, bishops, rabbis, mullahs, gurus, and other defenders of the faith. In politics and economics dissident minorities are excluded from the corridors of power. There is no forum available for them, no opportunity to participate in open inquiry. Thus the so-called Higher Truth, so protected from investigation, lies beyond contest. A similar closed syndrome can be found in philosophy or science when it is held to be immune to free inquiry. Thomism, Calvinism, and Marxist-Leninism were considered official doctrines at various times in history by those who defended them in the name of an entrenched power elite. The same is true for Lysenkoism under Stalin or racist theories under the Nazis. In the battle for civil liberties in democratic societies political power has been wrested from repressive oligarchies. Unfortunately, the right to know has not been universally recognized as a basic human right in all societies, and there are wide areas—especially in religion and morality—that are still held to be immune to criticism.

The first principle of humanism is a commitment to free inquiry in every field of human endeavor. This means that any effort to prevent the free mind from exercising its right to pose questions and initiate inquiry is unwarranted.

But which methods of inquiry should be used? How do we evaluate truth claims? Philosophers have long debated the question "What is truth?" How we appraise knowledge claims depends on the subject matter under investigation, be it science, mathematics, philosophy, ethics, politics, economics, history, or the arts. Let it suffice for now to outline a minimal set of epistemological criteria that cuts across the various disciplines, without any lengthy explication in defense.[1] I will focus on skepticism, the scientific method, and critical intelligence.

Skepticism is a vital methodological principle of inquiry. I refer not to negative or nihilistic skepticism, which rejects the very possibility of attaining reliable knowledge, but positive, selective skepticism. This principle of skepticism implies that the reliability of a hypothesis, theory, or belief is a function of the grounds, evidence, or reasons by which it is supported. If a claim is not justified by objective validation or verification, we ought to be cautious in holding fast to it. The amount of supporting evidence will vary with the subject under scrutiny.

Probabilism points to the degree of certainty by which we are willing to ascertain truth claims. We should not attribute to any belief absolute infallibility. We should be prepared to admit that we may be mistaken. Beliefs should be taken as hypotheses: they are tentative or hypothetical depending upon the degree of evidence or the validity of the arguments used to support them.

Fallibilism is a principle which indicates that even when a claim is thought to be well supported, we should nonetheless be prepared to modify our beliefs if new arguments or evidence arise in the future which show either that we were in error or that our truths were only partial and limited. This applies in fields of formal knowledge, such as mathematics, as much as to experimental domains of inquiry. The skeptic should have an open mind about all questions and not seek to close responsible inquiry in any field. If after investigation there is insufficient evidence, the skeptic may say that the claim is unlikely, improbable, or false, or if further investigation is possible, he may wish to suspend judgment and admit that he does not know. Agnosticism, in this respect, is a meaningful option. We should be prepared to exercise doubt about a wide range of belief claims which we have little expectation at present of resolving. Skepticism is thus an essential method used in science, technology, philosophy, religion, politics, morality, and ordinary life.

But the question may be asked: *Which* method should be used to warrant beliefs? What are the criteria of confirmation and validity? Without attempting to resolve this question fully here, let me suggest the following criteria:

First, we should appeal to *experience* in all areas in which it is pertinent to do so. By this I mean observation, evidence, facts, data—preferably involving some intersubjective grounds that can be replicated or certified. Purely subjective or private paths to truth need not be arbitrarily rejected, but, on the other hand, they are not admissible to the body of knowledge unless they can be reliably corroborated by others. This empirical test is fundamental. But if we are to draw any inferences from it then it must refer to experiential claims that are open to public scrutiny, not only in ascertaining whether they occurred but also in interpreting their likely causes.

Second, if an experience cannot be duplicated, there might be circumstantial evidence or at least *predictable* results by which we can evaluate its adequacy. In other words, our beliefs are forms of behavior, and they can be tested—at least in part—by their observed consequences. This is an experimental criterion used not only in laboratories but also in everyday life when we appraise beliefs not simply by what people say but by what they do.

Third, we use a *rational* test of deductive coherence, judging our theories or beliefs by relation to those we have already accepted as reliable. Hypotheses and theories cannot be viewed in isolation from other knowledge we believe to be true. They are logically consistent or inconsistent with it, and are judged by the criterion of validity. We can see this test at work not only in mathematical, logical, and formal systems but also in science and ordinary affairs when we test beliefs by their internal consistency.

The preceding criteria are used most explicitly in the sciences, where hypothetical-deductive methods prevail and where we formulate hypotheses and test them by their experimental adequacy and logical coherence. Science is not a method of knowing available only to an esoteric coterie of experts; similar standards of reasoning are employed in common everyday life when we are faced with problems and wish to resolve practical questions.

The terms *reason, rationality,* and *reasonableness* have sometimes been used to describe the general methodology that humanists have advocated: that is, we should test truth claims objectively as far as we can, and if claims cannot pass the tests of reason (broadly conceived to include experience and rationality), we should either reject them or suspend judgment. We face an epistemological crisis today, for with the increasing specialization of knowledge, experts often restrict their use of objective methods of inquiry to their own fields of competency and are unwilling to extend reason to other areas of human knowledge. What is at issue here is whether we can apply the powers of reason so that they will have some influence on the totality of beliefs.

Perhaps the best terminology to describe objectivity in testing truth claims is *critical intelligence*. This means that we must use our powers of critical analysis and observation to evaluate carefully questions of belief. We first need to define what is at stake. Here clarity in meaning is essential. We need to be clear about what we wish to know and what is at issue. We need to ask: What alternative explanations are offered? We formulate hypotheses and develop beliefs that help solve our puzzlement. The salient point is that only objective evidence and reasons will suffice to evaluate alternative hypotheses.

What is distinctive about humanism as a eupraxsophy is that

it wishes to extend the methods of objective inquiry to all areas of life, including religious, philosophical, ethical, and political concerns that are often left unexamined. There has been extensive research into specialized areas of scientific knowledge, particularly since technological discoveries have provided an enormous boon to human welfare; however, powerful forces have often distrusted and indeed prevented free inquiry into the foundations of social, moral, and religious systems. The crux of the matter is whether objective methods of inquiry can be applied to these vital areas of human concern. If critical intelligence were to supplant blind appeals to authority, custom, faith, or subjectivity, it could radically transform society. Free thought can be threatening to the privileged bastions of the status quo.

No doubt a basic point of contention between humanism and theism is precisely here: the application of scientific methods, rationalism, and critical intelligence to evaluate transcendental claims. The critics of humanism maintain that it excludes, almost by definition, claims to a transcendental realm. This, I submit, is not the case; for the humanist is willing to examine any responsible claim to truth. The burden of proof, however, rests with the believer to specify clearly the conditions under which his beliefs may be falsified. The humanist requests that whatever is under examination be carefully defined. God-talk is generally vague, ambiguous, even unintelligible. The humanist next wishes to know how the believer would justify its truth. If a meaningful claim is introduced, it needs to be corroborated. This means that private, mystical, or subjective claims to revelation or divine presence or mere declarations by ecclesiastical authorities that something is true are inadmissible unless they can be intersubjectively confirmed. We cannot exclude on a priori grounds any insights derived from literature, poetry, or the arts. These express enduring human interests. We only ask that they be analyzed carefully and tested objectively. Aesthetic experience is a rich part of human experience, and it may provide a wealth of insight and inspiration. Any knowledge about the world drawn from these sources, however, requires careful evaluation.

The humanist is open to the subtle nuances of human experience, but he insists that we use our powers of critical judgment to appraise the claims to truth. In this sense, he draws upon the tested knowledge and the best available wisdom of the day. He will accept the claims of others—even if he has not personally scrutinized each of these claims—but only if he is assured that those claims have been warranted by objective methods, and that if he or someone else had the time, energy, and training he could scrutinize the procedures used to corroborate the findings. The methods of critical intelligence apply not only to descriptive truth claims, where we seek to describe and explain natural processes, but also to normative judgments, where we formulate eupraxic recommendations in the various domains of human action.

A COSMIC WORLD VIEW

Humanist eupraxsophy does not simply assert a method of inquiry based upon the methods of science; it also seeks to use the sciences to interpret the cosmos and the place of the human species within it. The humanist thus attempts to make some kind of generalized sense of reality. Speculative metaphysics is in disrepute today, and rightly so if it seeks to derive universal principles about reality from purely intuitive or metaphorical methods. The primary source for obtaining knowledge about nature should be human experience. It is within the various disciplines of scientific research and scholarship that reliable hypotheses and theories are elaborated and tested. If this is the case, then any comprehensive view of nature must draw heavily upon the scientific understanding of the day. Since science is a rapidly expanding body of knowledge, there are ongoing modifications of principles, hypotheses, and theories. There may at times be fundamental shifts in outlook, in which longstanding paradigms are altered, as for example, the fundamental transformation of Newtonian science by relativity theory and quantum mechanics. We note also the basic changes that have occurred in genetics, biology, psychology, the social sciences, and other fields of research in the twentieth century. There are times when we build up and elaborate a body of knowledge by a process of accumulation and addition. At other times there may be radical disruptions: novel theories may be introduced and tested, and they may fundamentally alter the prevailing outlook. One must be prepared to change a cosmic perspective in the light of new data and theories. We must be tentative in our formulations and prepared to revise theories in the light of new discoveries.

Unfortunately, scientists in specialized disciplines are often unaware of developments in other fields, and they may be unwilling or unable to relate their findings to domains of knowledge outside their competence or to develop a cosmic view. This is where philosophy enters: the philosopher should interpret the knowledge of one discipline and relate it to other fields. Philosophy, by definition, is general, for it is concerned with finding common methods, principles, postulates, axioms, assumptions, concepts, and generalizations used in a wide range of fields. Here I refer to the philosophy of science and to the methods of analysis and generalization by which it interprets the various sciences.

The great philosophers have always attempted to do this. Aristotle's *Metaphysics* provided a critical interpretation of the key concepts and categories underlying our knowledge of nature. Similarly, Descartes, Leibniz, Hume, Kant, Russell, Dewey, Whitehead, and others reflected upon and attempted to interpret the sciences of their day. We need to do the same today, though it may be far more difficult than in previous ages because of the immense proliferation of the sciences; it is difficult for any one mind to sum up the enormous bodies of specialties in some sort of interrelated whole. If we cannot as yet succeed in this ambitious venture, at the very least we can try in a more modest way. Using physics, astronomy, and the natural sciences, we can develop some cosmologies that explain the expanding universe. Using biology and genetics we can try to interpret the evolution of life. We can use psychology to understand human behavior, and we can draw upon anthropology, sociology, and the other social sciences to develop appropriate theories about sociocultural phenomena. This is an ongoing quest. We do not have a comprehensive theory of the universe at present. Nonetheless we do have kaleidoscopic pictures of nature that are based on the sciences.

What does humanist eupraxsophy tell us about the cosmos? Let us approach the question at first by negative definition, by indicating what is unlikely. There is insufficient evidence for the claim that there is a divine creator who has brought the universe into being by an act of will. The invoking of God as a cause of everything that is, is mere *postulation*, without sufficient evidence or proof. It is a leap outside nature. The concept of a transcendent supernatural being is unintelligible; the idea of a First Cause, itself uncaused, is contradictory. Even if the Big Bang theory in astronomy is useful in explaining the rapidly receding and expanding universe, this does not provide support for the claim that there was a Being who existed coterminous or antecedent to this explosion. The Big Bang may be the result of a random quantum fluctuation, not an intelligent plan.

To read into such a cosmological principle selective human qualities—intelligence, perfection, or personhood—is unwarranted. The universe does not manifest design; there is apparent regularity and order, but chance and conflict, chaos and disorder are also present. To describe the entire universe as *good* is an anthropomorphic rendering of nature to fit one's moral bias. If there is apparent good in the universe, there would also have to be apparent evil, at least from the standpoint of sentient beings, who at times devour one another in the struggle for survival or who encounter natural disasters that destroy them. If so, how can we reconcile evil with a provident deity? Theists are so overcome by the tragic character of human finitude that they are willing to project their deepest longings into a divine mind, and this enables them to transcend nothingness. For the theist the universe involves some teleological conception of salvation. Man, in some way, is at the center of creation; for God is endowed by man with human qualities, especially with a compassionate concern for our plight. God will save us if only we will devote ourselves completely to adoring Him, accept on the basis of faith that which passeth all human understanding, and obey His moral commandments as interpreted by His self-proclaimed emissaries on earth.

Much of the anthropomorphic character of the deity is derived from ancient texts held to be sacred and to have been revealed by God to specially appointed individuals. The Bible predicates the intervention of the Holy Ghost in history. Yet scientific and scholarly biblical criticism has made it abundantly clear that the Bible is a human document, a thousand-year-old record of the experiences of primitive nomadic and agricultural tribes living on the eastern shore of the Mediterranean. There is no evidence that Yahweh spoke to Abraham, Moses, Joseph, or any of the Old Testament prophets. The biblical accounts of their experiences are the records of Hebrew national existence, seeking to sustain itself by the myth of the "chosen people." These books have not been empirically validated; they express an ancient world view and the moral conceptions of a prescientific culture that invoked deities to sanctify its ideological aspirations.

The New Testament presents the incredible tale of Jesus, a man of whom we have very little historical knowledge. Obviously this is not an objective historical account. The "divinity" of Jesus has never been adequately demonstrated. Yet powerful churches have sought to inculcate the mythic story and to suppress dissent. The tales of Jesus' life and ministry expressed in the Four Gospels and the letters of Paul were written twenty to seventy years after his death. They are riddled with the contradictions implicit in an oral tradition. Defended by propagandists for a new mystery religion, the biblical accounts are hardly to be taken as dispassionate historical evidence for Jesus' divine origin. The tales of the so-called miracles and faith healings of Jesus are based on uncorroborated testimony by an unsophisticated people who were easily deceived. That the Jesus myth was elaborated by later generations and was eventually promulgated by powerful church institutions that dominated Europe for almost two millennia and still have inordinate influence on large sectors of the globe is evidence for the presence of a transcendental temptation within the human heart, which is ever ready to seize upon any shred of hope for an afterlife.

Similar skeptical criticism may be leveled against other supernatural religions. Islam is a religion based on the alleged revelations to Muhammad, received from on high through the archangel Gabriel, at first in caves north of Mecca and later in various other places. Careful reading of the literature about the origins of the Koran enables us to give alternative naturalistic explanations of Muhammad's ministry. He may have suffered from some form of epilepsy, which explains his trance states or swoons. He was able to convince others of his divine calling, and he used this ploy to achieve power. All of this is testimony to the gullibility of human beings and their willingness to abandon acceptable standards of rationality when they are confronted with claims to a Higher Truth. The same thing can be noted of the legions of saints, prophets, gurus, and shamans throughout history who have proclaimed divine revelations and have used their claims to delude and influence their followers.

Basic to the monotheistic approach is the belief in an afterlife. Is it possible for a "soul" to survive the death of the body? Jewish, Christian, and Muslim adherents fervently believe in the immortality of the soul, and Hindus, in its reincarnation from previous existences.

Unfortunately, the most resolute and objective investigations of claims of survival have shown them to be without empirical corroboration. Psychical researchers, parapsychologists, and paranormal investigators, for over a century, have produced reports of ghosts, spirits, apparitions, and poltergeists, but there is insufficient data to support the reality of discarnate existence, despite the legions of spiritualists, trance channelers, and past-life regressors who claim to be in touch with an unseen realm of spiritual reality. Although our fondest hopes and desires may *demand* life before birth or after death, the evidence points in the other direction. Even if it could be proved that something briefly survives the death of the biological body, there is no evidence of an eternal state of existence or of a blessed union with God. The evidence for survival is based on wishful thinking and is totally inconclusive. Death seems to be the natural state of all life forms, even though modern medical science and technology are able to ward off disease and prolong life. Humanism is thus skeptical about the entire drama of the theistic universe: that God exists and that we can achieve salvation in an afterlife.

But what picture of the universe does humanism provide as a substitute? Perhaps not one that slakes the existential yearnings of the desperate soul, but one that is more in accordance with the world as uncovered by science. What we have today is an ope-nended universe, perhaps ragged at the edges and with many gaps in our knowledge, but it is a picture supported by the best available evidence. At the present stage of human knowledge, the following general propositions seem true:

Objects or events within the universe have material explana-tions. All objects or events encountered have a physical char-acter. Matter, mass, and energy may, however, be organized on various levels, ranging from the minutest microparticles on the subatomic level in fields of energy to gigantic objects such as planets, moons, comets, stars, quasars, and galaxies.

We encounter within the universe order and regularity on the one hand and chaos and random fluctuations on the other.

Objects and events within the universe seem to be evolving. Change is an enduring trait of existing things. The cosmos as we presently understand it is something on the order of ten to twenty billion years old; it is expanding from what seems to have been a huge explosion. In any case, our planet is only one satellite of a minor star in the Milky Way, which is merely one galaxy among billions in the vast universe. What preceded the Big Bang, the physicists are not yet able to explain, and what will be the end of the universe—a whimper or a big crunch as matter implodes—is also difficult to say.

The universe is not, however, inanimate. There is some likelihood that organic life exists in other parts of the universe. The earliest known fossils uncovered on the earth are more than three billion years old. The most useful hypothesis to explain the diverse forms of life on our planet is that they evolved from common genetic material and split into diverse species. Evolution is a product of chance mutations, differential reproduction, and adaptation. The human species most likely evolved over a period of several million years, exhibiting processes that follow similar patterns in other species. Distinctive to human primates is the large cerebral cortex and the development of highly complex social systems in which tools are manipulated and signs and symbols function to enable linguistic communication. Genetics, biology, and psychology explain the emergence of human behavior and how and why we function the way we do. The social sciences are able to account for the development of the complex social institutions that help to satisfy basic human needs.

The study of culture demonstrates that individual members of the human species are physio-chemical biological systems genetically predisposed to certain forms of behavior, yet able to learn; they are influenced by environmental factors and capable of adaptive behavior. There seems to be a creative component to all forms of organic life—this is especially true of the human species. The human organism is able to respond to stimuli not only by conditioned behavior but by expressing creative impulses and demonstrating cognitive awareness. Humans, as products of nature, are able to understand the causes and conditions of their behavior, and they are able to intervene in the processes of nature and change them by discovery and invention. Formerly, the course of human evolution was largely unconscious and blind. We can now redirect to some extent by conscious effort the evolution of the species. Human behavior may be modified by imaginative effort and ingenuity. Human beings manifest rational choice. They are able to solve the problems encountered in living and thus, in part, to determine their futures. This is the message of the humanist outlook.

A LIFE STANCE

Men and women are capable of free choice. How much and to what extent has been hotly debated by philosophers, theologians, and scientists. Clearly, our behavior is limited or determined by the conditions under which we act. There are physiochemical, genetic, sociological, and psychological causes at work. Yet, in spite of these causal factors, we are consciously aware and we are capable of some teleonomic and preferential choice. Cognition can selectively direct our behavior.

"What ought I to choose?" and "How ought I to live?" are questions constantly raised. Are there any norms that humanism can offer to guide our conduct? Can we discover any enduring ends or goals? Is there a good which we ought to seek? Are there ethical standards of right and wrong? Is there a distinct set of ethical values and principles that may be said to be humanistic?

These are large questions, and I can only sketch in outline form what I consider to be the ethics of humanism.[2] Its critics maintain that humanism lacks proper moral standards, that it is permissive, and that it allows subjective taste and caprice to prevail. Without belief in God, these critics assert, an ethic of responsibility is impossible.

These charges are unfounded. They emanate from an abysmal ignorance of the history of philosophical ethics, for philosophers have demonstrated the possibility of an autonomous ethic in which moral obligations emerge.

By arguing that ethics is autonomous, I simply mean that it is possible to make moral judgments of good, bad, right and wrong independently of one's ultimate foundations; i.e., there is a fund of common moral decencies that can be developed in human experience. Yet humanist ethics does have foundations, and these are its eupraxsophy, which in the last analysis completes it; for when questions of "ultimate" obligation or "ultimate" moral purpose arise the theist falls back on God, whereas the humanist is skeptical of that claim and places his ethics in a naturalistic evolutionary universe that is devoid of purpose. The humanist life stance thus has its grounding in nature and human nature.[3]

There are at least two alternative approaches to the moral life: (1) transcendental theistic systems of morality; (2) humanist ethics. Let me state simply that if God does not exist and the so-called "sacred" texts are not divinely inspired but are the expressions of human culture at certain historical periods, then appeals to transcendental ethics can hardly serve as guides for conduct.

Interestingly, those systems which claim to deduce our moral obligations from a belief in God often promulgate contradictory codes of behavior, waging constant warfare about the legitimacy of rival priesthoods to interpret God's word properly. In any case, all systems of morality are humanly based; it is a question of which best serves the moral needs of humankind-theism or humanism.

What are the essential ingredients of the ethics of humanism? The humanist life stance has a clearly developed conception of what "good practice" and "right conduct" are. The ethics of humanism may be said to begin when men and women eat of the "god-forbidden fruit" of the tree of knowledge of good and evil.

Critical ethical inquiry enables us to transcend unquestioned customs, blind faith, or doctrinaire authority and to discover ethical values and principles. Humanists maintain that a higher state of moral development is reached when we go beyond unthinking habits to ethical wisdom: This includes an appreciation of the standards of excellence and an awareness of ethical principles and one's moral responsibilities to others.

The starting point for humanism is a response to the question "What is the meaning of life?" The theist is mired in the salvation myth, which he believes gives meaning to his mortal existence, and he cannot comprehend how human beings can find life meaningful or behave responsibly without it.

The quest for transcendent meaning is a futile endeavor, however, for there is no evidence that nature has some mysterious divine reality locked away, which, once revealed, will relieve us of the need to make our own choices or direct our own destinies.

Life has no hidden singular meaning per se. The promises of priests and other religious leaders to provide a path is often merely a deception perpetrated on gullible souls who lack the courage to summon their own resources to live fully. The quest for the Holy Grail is an escape from facticity, contingency, and finitude.

Humanists begin with the realization that the universe is a vast, impersonal system, impervious to their interests and needs, yet regard it as full of wonderful challenges and opportunities that enable them to create their own life-worlds. They realize that death is the inevitable fate of all biological creatures, that the central value is to fulfill and enhance life itself—to eat of the bountiful fruit of the tree of life—and that to enjoy its succulent flavors and fragrance can be intrinsically energizing and exciting.

To ask for *the* meaning of life, as if there were one magic key, makes no sense. Life is full of *plural meanings*, it can be abundant and overflowing with possibilities. The term *meaning* has significance only for sentient beings who are self-aware. The world of meaning is the field of nature and culture in which we discover things that are significant to us and in which we initiate our plans, actualize our projects, and create relationships that are of moral value.

Here then is the humanist life stance: humanists do not look upward to a heaven for a promise of divine deliverance. They have their feet planted squarely on Mother Earth, yet they have the Promethean fortitude to employ art, science, sympathy, reason, and education to create a better world for themselves and their fellow human beings.

From the standpoint of the individual, the summum bonum is worthwhile happiness. This is not a passive quest for release from the world, but the pursuit of an active life of adventure and fulfillment. There are so many opportunities for creative enjoyment that every moment can be viewed as precious; all fit together to make up a full and exuberant life which makes the world a better place.

A basic method for achieving the good life is the method of reason; we need to cultivate the capacity of critical intelligence in ethical inquiry and the knowledge of good and evil so that we can make sensible choices. For the humanist, practical wisdom is the ability to choose between alternatives after a process of deliberation, by appraising means and ends and estimating the costs and consequences of his choices for himself and others. For the theist the ultimate virtues are obedience to God's commandments, faith in his deliverance, and some form of worship. For the humanist the three basic virtues are (1) *courage*—the determination to overcome and prevail in spite of adversity; (2) *reason*—the use of critical intelligence to solve human problems and to understand nature; and (3) *compassion*—the moral awareness of the needs of others.

Historically philosophers have recognized that happiness is a basic good of life, though they have long argued about its nature. Hedonists have maintained that happiness is the attainment of pleasure and the avoidance of pain; self-actualizers have said that it is the fulfillment of our potentialities. I submit that both ideas are involved in the good life, that we want enriched enjoyment *and* creative realization of our talents. If an individual is to achieve a state of happiness, he needs to develop a number of excellences. I will only list these, without explication: the capacity for autonomous choice and freedom, creativity, intelligence, self-discipline, self-respect, high motivation, good will, an affirmative outlook, good health, the capacity to enjoy pleasure, and aesthetic appreciation.[4] Men and women do not five in isolation but fulfill their highest ideals in concert with others.

One also needs to develop an appreciation for what we may call "the common moral decencies." I submit that deeply rooted in our history as socio-biological beings are our potentialities for moral behavior. There are many ethical principles that reason can discover: (1) *integrity*—being truthful, keeping promises, being sincere and honest; (2) *trustworthiness*—fidelity, dependability; (3) *benevolence*—good will, absence of malice, consensual sexual relations, beneficence; and (4) *fairness*—gratitude, accountability, justice, tolerance, peacefulness, and cooperation. These principles are cross-cultural. They are widely recognized by human beings of different historical epochs and cultures. In particular, reflective ethical awareness demonstrates the fact that we have responsibilities to ourselves: to fulfill our talents and to develop self-respect and self-restraint. But we also have responsibilities to others, especially within the family: parents to children and children to parents; husbands to wives, and vice versa; and relatives to each other. We also have obligations that arise among friends. There are in addition moral duties that emerge within our circle of interaction within our communities. And last but not least, we have an obligation to the entire world community. I am only stating these ethical principles or moral decencies now, without any extended defense, but I submit that a person with a reflective and developed moral awareness can discover standards of excellence, decency, and responsibility.

The ethics of humanism stands in sharp contrast to theistic doctrines. The end of the good life is to realize the worthiness of life itself, to fulfill our dreams and aspirations, plans and projects here and now. It involves not only a concern for one's own life (some self-interest is not wicked but essential) and the fulfillment of one's own desires, needs, and interests, but also a concern for the well-being of others, an altruistic regard for the communities where one interacts. And it extends eventually to all within the planetary society.

Humanist ethics does not rest on arbitrary caprice but on reflective choice. Ethical principles and values are rational: they are relative to human interests and needs. But this does not mean that they are subjective, nor are they beyond the domain of skeptical critical inquiry. Our principles and values can be tested by their consequences in action.

What is vital in humanist eupraxsophy is that humanists are not overwhelmed by the "tragic" character of the human condition; they must face death, sorrow, and suffering with courage. They have confidence in the ability of human beings to overcome alienation, solve the problems of living, and develop the capacity to share the goods of life and empathize with others. The theist has a degraded view of man, who, beset with original sin, is incapable of solving life's problems by himself and needs to look outside of the human realm for divine succor. The humanist accepts the fact that the human species has imperfections and limitations and that some things encountered in existence are beyond repair or redress. Yet even so, he believes the best posture is not to retreat into fear and trembling before injustice or the unknown forces of nature, but to exert his intelligence and courage to deal with these matters. It is only by a resolute appraisal of the human condition, based on reason and a cosmic world view, that the humanist's life stance seems most appropriate. He is unwilling to fall to his knees before the forces of nature but will stand on his own feet to battle evil and build a better life for himself and his fellow human beings. In other words, he expresses the highest heroic virtues of the Promethean spirit: audacity and nobility! And he has also developed moral sensibilities about the needs of others.

SOCIAL POLITY

Humanism is not concerned only with the life stance of the individual—however basic this is as an alternative to theism; it is also concerned with the achievement of the good society. The early Greek philosophers had discussed the nature of justice. For Plato justice can best be seen writ large in the state, but it is also seen in the life of the individual soul. Justice involves the principles of harmony, order, and reason. For Aristotle ethics and politics are related. He is concerned with the happiness of the individual, but the more comprehensive art is politics, for it deals with questions about the polity of governments and good constitutions. Historically the philosophers Machiavelli, Hobbes, Spinoza, Locke, Hume, Rousseau, Comte, Hegel, Dewey, and Russell have been vitally concerned with the nature of the just society.

Does humanism today have concrete recommendations for the social polity? Surely humanist eupraxsophy must deal with the well-being of humanity on the larger scale, for if the ultimate good is life here and now, then this cannot be achieved by the solitary individual alone but only in concert with others within a larger sociocultural context. It is clear that eupraxsophy does not simply delineate a theoretical intellectual position but also has something to say about social practice. Indeed, for Karl Marx social praxis was essential for humanism. Abstract atheism was insufficient in itself; one needed to move on to a positive program of social reform. The next stage in human history, he said, was communism, that is, the transformation of the class system and of the conditions of production. What was unique in Marx's

thought was that philosophy was to go beyond the merely contemplative mode of understanding political and social philosophy to the practical implementation of its ideals. In this sense,
Marxist philosophy was a eupraxsophy. Regrettably, Marx's theories, which were grounded in Hegelian categories, seem to have
submerged the individual before the dialectical processes of history; and the decisive forces on the historical stage were economic and social institutions. In Marx's and Engel's sociological
interpretation of history, the forces and relationships of production are the foundation for social change; religious, political,
moral, intellectual, scientific, and aesthetic factors were derivative and in the superstructure of society.

One can raise fundamental questions about whether Marx
was a humanist and whether his humanism was betrayed by
some latter-day Marxists who misinterpreted his writings. Surely
Marx was a secular humanist in the sense that he rejected an ide-
alistic-theist Weltanschauung. He was committed to a material-
istic view of nature and denied the existence of divine salvation.
He wished to use science (as he understood it) to reconstruct
social conditions and to contribute to human progress. Moreover,
he had a compassionate concern for ameliorating the life of the
ordinary worker and emancipating him from alienated labor and
oppression. The early Marx of the *Economic and Philosophic
Manuscripts of 1844* seemed to express the highest humanistic
values of freedom and creativity.[5] In this sense he is within the
great tradition of historic humanist philosophy, an heir to the
ideals of the Enlightenment, for he wished to use reason to solve
social problems, and he had some confidence in the ability of
man to do so.

There has been a deep split within contemporary humanist
eupraxia between some forms of Marxism and liberalism. Many
philosophers in Eastern Europe considered themselves to be
Marxist-humanists, as distinct from Leninist-Stalinists. And
there had been an irreconcilable rift in the West between democ-

ratic socialist parties and totalitarian communist ones. The central issue concerns democracy, for an indelible feature of humanism is its emphasis on *freedom*. The good society must seek to maximize freedom of choice and the autonomy of the individual as a basic value, and this cannot be sacrificed at the altar of the collective. This has been the first principle of classical liberalism—as expressed by Locke, Mill, and the Utilitarians—and it cannot be compromised. The pragmatic political philosophers John Dewey and Sidney Hook have attempted to accommodate both the individualism of liberalism and the sociality of Hegelian philosophy. The individual cannot live in isolation, for he interacts with others in society and culture. But what are the appropriate dimensions of individual freedom?

For the liberal democratic humanist it is first and foremost freedom of thought and conscience—philosophical, religious, intellectual, scientific, political, and moral freedom. This includes free speech, freedom of the press, the freedom to form voluntary associations and to pursue one's life style as one sees fit so long as one does not harm or limit the freedom of others. In specific terms, this means that the full range of civil liberties must be recognized by the just society, including the right to dissent and the legal right to oppose the policies of the government. This entails a commitment to political democracy: the right of the people to form political parties, to elect the officials of government, to determine the policies and programs of the state, to have some means to redress grievances, to be immune from arbitrary arrest and punishment, to be entitled to a fair trial and due process. Representative democracy bases its decisions on majority rule with the full protection of minority rights. Democracy also cherishes as basic values diversity, pluralism, creativity, and the uniqueness of individual citizens and groups in society. It is the compromise of these principles by some overzealous disciples of Marxism in the past, who were willing to use any means to achieve their ends—including revolutionary violence and state terror—that clearly demarcates totalitarian Marxism from democratic humanism. And it is for that reason clearly the case that Leninist-Stalinism is not a full humanism because it abandoned the central ethical value of individual freedom. Hopefully, Stalinism has given way and Lenin's heirs will become more democratic in their approach. Only time will tell.

Humanists can disagree about many things in the political and social sphere. Humanism is not a dogmatic creed. We cannot identify humanism with specific candidates or party platforms, in a particular period. Honest men and women often differ about what ought to be done. We can dispute about policies in the economic and political sphere: "Should there be high or low interest rates or none?" "Should taxes be on consumption or income?" "How can we increase productivity and not despoil the environment?" and so on. Humanists share with orthodox Christians and Jews any number of social ideals, and they may support common programs of political reform or stability. Humanists may differ among themselves on any number of concrete proposals. Such disagreement may be healthy, for there is not only one road to truth or virtue. We are all fallible. Humanism thus does not have a doctrinaire political platform on which it stands. Any effort to politicize humanism in a narrow sectarian way is unfortunate; one should not read political or economic conservatives out of the humanist fold. Nor should one ally humanism simply with socialism or free-market economic systems; the policies and programs that seem wise in one generation may give way to the experience of the next. The earlier identification of many idealistic humanists with left-wing socialism has been broken by the recognition that one should not compromise democratic freedoms or abandon incentive, which is so essential to expanding production. Many libertarians today, interested in defending freedom in the economic sphere, claim to be humanistic. Others believe that the wisest course of social polity is a mixture of welfare (socialist) and free-market (capitalist) policies.

Humanist eupraxia in regard to social polity thus should focus on the *basic values and principles* that all humanists share. What are some of the basic principles of humanist eupraxia as we enter the twenty-first century? The first commitment of the humanist, I submit, must be to the *method of intelligence* (as John Dewey argues in his definition of liberalism) as the most reliable way of solving social problems.[6] This means that social policies should be considered hypotheses based on the findings of the best empirical research of the day and tested by their consequences in action. The wisest and most sensible method of political governance and social change is by *democratic methods of persuasion.* Our ultimate reliance in a democracy must be on a fully informed citizenry as the chief source of power and decision making. The broader ideal here is the need to encourage widespread participation by the people in all the institutions of society in which they live, work together, and function. How this works out depends on the specific institutions. Here we are talking about political, economic, and social democracy.

If the methods of intelligence and democratic participation are to succeed, we need a well-educated and intelligent public. Thus, *opportunity for education* must be made available to all individuals in society; the right to knowledge is not only a basic human right but is also the key instrument by which society can best solve its problems. By expanding the ranges of cultural appreciation of all citizens, we contribute to our own moral, intellectual, and aesthetic development.

A central value for humanism and democracy is tolerance; a just society will allow alternative points of view and a plurality of life styles, beliefs, and moral values, all existing side by side. The chief method of resolving differences should be wherever possible the *peaceful negotiation of differences and compromise,* not force or violence.

A democratic society is one that recognizes the obligation to provide the opportunity and means for all individuals to *satisfy their basic economic and cultural needs.* Thus, an open democratic society will attempt to redress gross inequities in income and provide for the satisfaction of the basic minimal needs for those who are unable, through no fault of their own, to do so. I am referring here to policies of social welfare, unemployment and social security insurance, and aid to the handicapped and disadvantaged. This involves providing both economic and cultural opportunities so that individuals can participate in the democratic society and develop as self-reliant, autonomous, and productive citizens.

The just society will seek *to end discrimination* based on race, gender, creed, sexual orientation, physical handicap, ethnicity, or economic background and accord all of its citizens equal rights. It will provide women with full equality under the law. It will recognize the rights of children.

The preceding is only a thumbnail sketch of some of the principles of humanist social eupraxia. Heretofore, this has been interpreted as applying only to local communities or nation-states, and efforts have been made to democratize these from within. The world has reached such a level of economic and political interdependence today that it is no longer possible to resolve many problems concerning humanity on the local or national level alone. Thus, we need to develop an appreciation for universal (or general) human rights and apply them to all comers of the globe and all members of the human family. We need to build an *ethical commitment to the world community as our highest moral devotion.* There are conservative and reactionary nationalistic, separatist, and ethnic forces throughout the world that oppose this development. Yet it is central, I submit, to the next stage of human civilization.

NOTES

1. I have discussed criteria of meaning and proof in detail in the following books: *The Transcendental Temptation* (*op. cit.*), *Decision and the Condition of Man* (Seattle: University of Washington Press, 1965); and *The Skeptic's Handbook of Parapsychology* (Amherst, N.Y.: Prometheus Books, 1985).

2. I have provided more detail in *Forbidden Fruit: The Ethics of Humanism* (Amherst, N.Y.: Prometheus Books, 1988); *Decision and the Condition of Man* (op. cit.); and *Exuberance: The Philosophy of Happiness* (Los Angeles: Wilshire Books, 1977).

3. The term life stance was first introduced by Harry Stopes-Roe, "Humanism as a Life Stance," *Free Inquiry* 8, no. 1 (Winter 1987/88).

4. For a full discussion, see *Forbidden Fruit*, Chapter 4.

5. Karl Marx, *Economic and Philosophic Manuscripts of 1844* (New York: International Publishers, 1964).

6. John Dewey, *Liberalism and Social Action*, (New York: Capricorn Books, 1955); *The Public and Its Problems* (New York: Henry Holt and Co., 1927); *Freedom and Culture* (New York: Capricorn Books, 1939).

III. The Definition of Religion

THEISM AND THE SACRED

Our discussion thus far is prefatory to my assertion that humanism should not be construed as a religion but as a *euprax-sophy* and that those who label humanism a *religion* or *religious* are mistaken. As we have seen, humanism entails a method of inquiry, a cosmic world view, a life stance, and a social polity. It does not make spiritual or sacred claims about the nature of reality. Thus, it is not a religion in any fair definition of that term.

If humanism is *not* a religion, can we say more precisely what *is* a religion? There are at least two major approaches to defining a religion: in terms of content or of function. No doubt an element of definition-mongering enters into the entire dispute. The underlying argument concerns how widely the term *religion* should be applied, and important persuasive elements have entered into all such definitions. *Religion* surely applies, for example, to Judaism, Christianity, Islam, and Hinduism, but can it be stretched to include all the forms of religiosity in Asia—Confucianism and Zen Buddhism, for example? Does it apply to the multifarious primitive beliefs and practices described by anthropologists? Does it apply to animism or to later polytheistic belief systems such as we find in the Homeric poems of the Greeks? More crucially, can *religion* be extended to incorporate classical philosophical schools, such as Epicureanism and Stoicism, or modern-day Marxism and humanism, which according to the functionalists have taken over some of the functions of traditional religion? As I have already indicated, one has to draw the linguistic line somewhat more narrowly or else the term *religion* loses any distinctive significance and may be applied to almost anything and everything.

The problem of proper definition arises in other areas as well. For example, it intrudes in efforts to define *democracy*, *socialism*, *liberalism*, *conservatism*, and contending parties dispute as to what should be included or excluded from the rubric of such terms. Hitler called his party the National Socialist German Workers' Party (Nazi), but it was hardly socialist. Many communist regimes have called themselves "democratic republics," but they were hardly democratic. Similarly, liberals and conservatives are at loggerheads about the definitions of true liberalism and conservatism.

The dispute more fundamentally concerns the nature of definition itself. What is a definition supposed to accomplish? On the one hand, the definition of a noun is descriptive, for it designates objects, events, beliefs, or practices that bear some similarity to each other and that can be classified under a common heading. Here, there are some differential characteristics that would enable us to apply a term to a range of phenomena. Terms have meanings and uses in a specific language stock, so that anyone who employs a term will be understood and can communicate. If we wish to define a word we turn to a dictionary: its meaning is determined by seeing what is commonly meant by it and how it is used. Thus the meaning of a linguistic term is determined not only by ascertaining the object or belief to which the term refers in the real world but how it is conventionally understood to apply by those who use the term.

Actually, it is not the specific word in a language stock that is central but the concept or idea which the term expresses. For example, the term *good* in English has its cognate in the French *bon* and in the German *gut*, though it is sometimes difficult to find a direct translation between languages since there may be subtle nuances in different language stocks. Admittedly, abstract terms are especially complex; some critics, such as G. E. Moore, cannot find the clear reference to the term *good* in any universe of discourse.[1] To make the point more precisely: How does one translate the German term *Weltschmerz* into English—as "world pain," "metaphysical dread," "anxiety," "weariness of life," "pessimism," or "melancholy"? We understand its meaning in German, yet any translation between languages seems to miss something.

This points to the fact that words may be laden with a variety of complex meanings, nuances, and functions: terms are not simply descriptive but also have emotive, aesthetic, prescriptive, and performatory connotations and functions.

Moreover, to define a term in any given language stock ordinarily used in one way by extending it metaphorically, however slightly, involves some redefinition, and this implies a kind of legislative element. The poet is able to leapfrog metaphors, adding to the richness of language. One of T. S. Eliot's eloquent metaphors reads: "This is the way the world ends/Not with a bang but a whimper." Here *whimper* has been extended beyond its normal context, but it is a beautiful application. Constant changes are going on in any language system. Languages are living vehicles for expressing ideas and communicating meanings; they will always be stretched to cover yet new experiences. Where adequate terms are not available in ordinary language, new ones have to be introduced or invented.

The term *religion* is not simply a descriptive term but involves a normative intent in which elements may be reclassified. There is a persuasive element involved in any kind of redefinition. Where we draw the line is often arbitrary. This is especially the case with terms that are newly coined and introduced into the language stock. Take the term *automobile*, a new term which is derived from the French *auto* and *mobile*, referring to that which contains the means of propulsion from within—self-propelling. It refers today to landbased, motor-driven vehicles or cars; it does not apply to airplanes, which are also "auto-mobiles" in a sense, since they contain the means of propulsion by burning fuel and propelling themselves. *Airplane* is derived from Latin and Greek roots, *aero* and *pianos*, "wandering in air" from Greek *aer* (air) plus *pianos* (wandering). *Airplane* refers to fixed-wing aircraft heavier than air driven by a propeller or a high-velocity jet engine and supported by the dynamic reaction of the air against its wings. We understand that motor vehicles or cars are different from airplanes, though we could have a word that includes both these and others under the same rubric: boats and trains are auto-mobiles as well, though there are differences. So definition involves distinction; although objects and the words that apply to them have similarities, they also have differences.

What about the term *religion*? Should it be used so widely that it blurs real differences among the beliefs and practices to which it is applied? I submit that the distinctive force of the term *religion* involves some belief *in a divine or sacred reality and some binding relationship of worship or devotion to it*. Under this definition, humanism is excluded from the rubric.

Etymologically, the term derives from the Latin *religio* or *relligio*. The meaning of these terms has been the subject of intense controversy ever since Cicero. Two alternative derivations have been given: *relegere* (to gather together, collect, hence to read or collect at a glance) and *religare* (to bind back or fasten) from *ligare* (to bind). According to Cicero, "men were called 'religious' from *relegere*, because they reconsidered carefully and, as it were, went over again in thought all that appertained to the worship of the gods."[2] This is questionable. An alternative derivation is from *religare*, to fasten or bind, which is adopted by the Roman author and Christian apologist Lactantius.[3] Servius and St. Augustine also took *religare* as the source of the word *religion* and used it to refer to the monastic life with its binding rules.[4,5] For Lactantius the word refers to the idea of an obligation that binds a person to an invisible god.

Many modern writers accept the second etymological view. The *Oxford English Dictionary* (1971 edition) gives its definition of religion as follows:

1. A state of life bound by monastic vows; the condition of one who is a member of a religious order.
2. A particular monastic or religious order or rule.
3. Action or conduct indicating a belief in, reverence for, and desire to please a divine ruling power; the exercise or practice of rites or observances implying this.
4. A particular system of faith and worship.
5. Recognition on the part of man of some higher unseen power as having control of his destiny, and as being entitled to obedience, reverence, and worship . . . .

Many definitions have since been proposed. *Webster's Ninth New Collegiate Dictionary* defines as the first two criteria of *religion* "the service and worship of God or the supernatural" and "a commitment or devotion to religious faith or observance."

It is thus a mistake, I submit, to apply the term *religion* to all human beliefs and practices encountered in all cultures. It is especially an error to apply it to humanism.

Numerous anthropologists and sociologists who have studied primitive belief systems have sought to apply the term *religion* to certain types of behavior encountered in these cultures, which are also discovered within the orthodox religions surviving to the present day. They focus on the "spiritual" and the "sacred." Thus E. E. Taylor proposed as a minimal definition of *religion* "the belief in spiritual beings."[6] This is no doubt an incomplete definition, since it leaves out practices; religions do not involve only belief. In many primitive cultures, ritual, not belief or dogma, is primary. Sir James G. Frazer's famous definition in *The Golden Bough* refers to religion as "a propitiation or conciliation of powers superior to man which are believed to direct and control the course of nature and of human life."[7]

Others, such as E. Crawley,[8] have said that what seems essential to the primitive mind is the "awe of the sacred"; that is, that there is something in nature usually hidden, mysterious, unseen, and secret, hence considered divine, which is held to control the events of this world. This sacred being or beings have power and are adamant in some way. It is thought that one can deal with the contingent and tragic sorrows of life by means of ritual and prayer, and thus propitiate the sacred and cause it to assist us. Many primitive religions also express forms of animism, the belief that inanimate objects have spirits or consciousness and influence us as well.

Emile Durkheim's comparative definition of religion, based on studies of both primitive and modern religious institutions, defines religion as "a unified system of beliefs and practices relative to sacred things, that is to say, things that are set apart and forbidden—beliefs and practices which unite into one single social community called the church, all those who adhere to them."[9] Although this definition is broad enough to include both primitive and modern religions, it does not include purely philosophical or scientific beliefs or practices. Anthropologist Anthony F. C. Wallace concludes: "It is the premise of every religion—and this premise is religion's *defining characteristic*—that souls, supernatural beings and supernatural forces exist. Furthermore, there are certain minimal categories of behavior which, in the context of the supernatural premise, are always found in association with one another and . . . are the substance of religion itself."[10]

A DEFINITION PROPOSED

I tend to agree with these definitions of religion. Religions postulate a deep division of reality into two separate realms: the profane and the sacred. The first is the natural and material world of everyday life, a world that we encounter in experience, endure, enjoy, or suffer; it is the world of brute facticity directly perceived by our sense organs and understood by rational inference and explanation. The second is the unknown world beyond, which transcends the present capacities of acquaintance or understanding; it lies hidden and is mysterious. We have not as yet fully plumbed its depths or fathomed its true nature. The paradox we face is that human beings are often unable to cope with or comprehend the profane world fully—it is a place of joy and sorrow, achievement and failure, the stage where the drama of life unfolds. And so another world is postulated.

It is apparent that large areas of the universe are unknown to human beings. What we have learned about nature is only a small part of what may be known. We may even be limited in our knowledge by the kinds of sense organs and brain we have evolved, by the kinds of data that we experience, and the inferences we derive from them. The range of our understanding is limited by the fact that anything known must make some discernible *difference* in the world. Kant distinguished between the phenomenal world, limited to our perceptual experience, and the noumenal world, of which we can say nothing concrete—that which is understood and that which is still unintelligible. The history of knowledge demonstrates that what is unknown in one age may become comprehensible in the next. Science enables us to discover causal hypotheses and to test them. It enables us to convert the unknown, which was formerly masked in mystery and unintelligibility, into the known: the causes of a strange disease, a violent storm, volcano, earthquake, or flood. Conversely, good fortune or a victory is taken by religious believers as a sign of divine favor, bestowed on men and women by some unseen power. We know now that many such events can be given natural explanations, and yet large areas remain unknown.

The distinctive mark of the religious consciousness is that, instead of remaining skeptical about the uncharted regions of the universe, it believes that we possess a glimmer of light about a transcendent universe. A teleological purpose is read into the unknown depths of reality. More explicitly, the religious person designates this as *sacred and divine and holds it in veneration and awe.*

1. The first criterion of religion (whether primitive or theistic) is the belief that there is some realm of being that transcends experience or reason, that this realm is sacred, numinous or holy, and that it is related to the world as its ultimate cause or final purpose.

2. The second part of the religious consciousness is the belief that human beings have some obligation to the sacred. A religion is thus not simply a system of beliefs or a creed that can be memorized and recited, but is also a set of practices or rituals that are believed to put us into some sort of relationship with the sacred.

I am using the term *sacred* in a broad sense, for it has many different interpretations. "The sacred" has the following characteristics:

(a) it is hidden, mysterious, miraculous, ultimately transcendent.

(b) It is the cause of the world we know, as ground or creator, and it has superhuman powers, whether beneficent or demonic.

(c) Our belief-states and practices will, if properly expressed, put us in a satisfactory relationship with the sacred. This generally involves rituals, rites, prayers, and music, and may include dances, sacrifices, and other supplicative and propitiatory ceremonies.

The hidden, mysterious, or sacred may take many forms. It may refer to spirits, the souls of the dead, God, gods and goddesses, or a range of other occult forces. It may include—as in the Roman Catholic faith—the Trinity, angels, the saints, and the Virgin Mary. It may be peopled by the spirits of our ancestors, who exert influence on our lives and require continual obedience, or by threatening or malefic beings.

Moreover, the ways of the gods are not clearly comprehensible by mere mortals. While we may understand some of God's way—which he may or may not have revealed to someone at some time in history, depending upon the particular religion—much is still hidden, beyond reason, and "passeth all understanding." Central to the religious attitude is the "feeling of absolute dependence" (Schleiermacher's definition of religion): that is, the sense that our existence is completely dependent upon and controlled by forces beyond our understanding. Our own efforts pale to insignificance in the face of the vast universe.

Similarly, the kinds of rites and rituals performed vary from culture to culture: the gesticulated dance of frenzied ecstasy of a Sufi mystic; the rituals of a pious Jew who wears a yarmulke, prayer shawl, and phylacteries for his daily prayer; the Roman Catholic who "takes" communion during a ceremony conducted by a priest in which wine and a wafer are mysteriously transformed into the blood and the body of Christ; the Muslim who fasts during the month of Ramadan and prays five times a day facing Mecca; and the Christian fundamentalist who sings hymns and may "speak in tongues" on Sunday morning. Seneca and Iroquois Indians, Watusi and Zulu, Hindu Brahmins and sundry monks and shamen use different forms of ritual.

The idea of *binding* emerges, for religions become institutionalized and there are rules that bind the believer to obedience and prayer. All of this has subtle evocative, psychological, and sociological functions; even if there is no one on the other side of the transaction to hear our prayers, they do express our highest aspirations and give vent to our most poignant emotions.

It is clear that the humanist does not believe in the reality of the sacred; he is unwilling to attribute any kind of power to an unknown being and therefore assumes the posture of an agnostic. Although he may frame speculative hypotheses about unknown aspects of nature, he is willing to suspend judgment precisely because it is not yet known. He is especially dubious of the tendency of religious believers to project their own imaginative fantasies into the unknown and to make up the shortcomings of this life by imagining that all is fulfilled in the next. The humanist is weary of the efforts to endow an unknown divine personhood with superhuman qualities. Theism is a presumptive exploitation of human longing which offers an idealized reconstruction of reality and imaginative wish-fulfillment. This being the case, the humanist is unwilling to engage in rituals to sway or propitiate unknown forces; he does not express any religious piety toward the unknown.

This does not mean that the humanist is without a sense of awe at the magnificence of the universe, as seen for example by the astronomer, nor that he fails to appreciate its grandeur, nor even that he is always free of fear about that which he cannot control. But his attitude does not involve reading into nature his fondest hopes or vain desires; he does not delude himself into believing that the totality of the cosmos has some ultimate and intimate relationship to him.

Religions manifest other characteristics beyond the two basic ones I have been discussing.

3. Of great significance is the solace that religion provides the individual, for it beckons him to some haven from the eternal flux. There would be no point in invoking the sacred if he did not believe that this would have efficacy in moving the gods to compassion or stimulating divine grace on his behalf. Even the resolve to suppress inner desires enables some devout souls to

achieve some measure of freedom from worldly strivings. The believer holds that everyone has a place in the divine scheme of things. The universe thus has a deeper spiritual reality (Hinduism). There may even be some purpose now being unfolded in accordance with some divine drama (Judaism, Christianity, Islam). Religion thus seeks to transcend feelings of impotence and finitude before an otherwise implacable universe. It promises satisfaction of our desires by placing them into the broader context of eternity. There is promise of spiritual reward for those who accept the religion—although religions differ about what the reward is. Religion thus speaks to the solitary individual, the lowest as well as the loftiest in the social order, and it offers some kind of psychological release. It may be spiritual joy or peace in this life, or the hope of eternal salvation in the next.

4. The traditional religions that have endured have powerful social dimensions; they express the collective lives of peoples. This does not deny the existence of private internalized religions of soliloquy, worked out theologically to satisfy a person's own idiosyncratic needs. But religions are preeminently social phenomena. In time, as the number of adherents grows, beliefs and practices are institutionalized. The dogma is clearly laid down. The appropriate rituals are codified and sanctified. These are transmitted from generation to generation. The rules and regulations of piety strictly govern the lives of the faithful. Taboos are proclaimed, obligations demanded. A sense of sin or guilt is inculcated in the young, thereby restraining any attempt to break the moral code. In highly structured authoritarian systems, deviations may be severely punished. The heretic or infidel is condemned as an outcast. The faithful are obedient servants of the Lord.

An institutionalized religion requires a priesthood, however loosely it may function. This involves a specially designated class of individuals who are entrusted with the sacred laws and who, through vows and training, devote their lives to spiritual pursuits. There may be a permanent priesthood and/or volunteer lay people to serve the church or temple at certain periods in their lives. Special places are designated as sacred ground, such as the city where the chief propagator of the faith was born, lived, or died. Houses of worship are consecrated, and the divine is thought to be present on sacred ground.

5. Fundamental to these religions is the belief that at one time in history the master or prophet received a revelation or enlightenment and transmitted it to his followers. Some inner truth, spiritual ecstasy, or way of life is promulgated in Hinduism, Taoism, and some other religions of Asia. In monotheistic religions, a specific communication is received by a prophet, mystic, disciple, or son of God, and is transmitted to humanity (Moses, Jesus, Muhammad). Such a message takes the explicit form of commandments governing the relations of individuals to one another and the community, and to God himself. We have only to think of the Ten Commandments, the Sermon on the Mount, or the Koranic code.

6. There is also a literature of "sacred" books. Their origins are often only dimly known. Passed down from distant times, they contain the message that the spiritual leader or god proclaims to the faithful. The literature is so revered that its interpreters pore over its passages, and every word or phrase may assume transcendent significance. The Torah is housed in a holy place and kissed by orthodox Jews when it is taken out during recital on the Sabbath and holy days. The Bible is revered by Christians as God's word. The Koran is said to have been spoken to Muhammad by the angel Gabriel. The Vedas are venerated by Hindus, and the Buddhists have their sacred texts. All these are taken by the devout as proclaiming absolute, final, fixed truths.

Secular humanism does not have any of these six characteristics of religion. Although humanism attempts to provide the individual with some help in achieving the good life, it is not as described in (3). Humanism does not promise ultimate release or eternal salvation. Humanism does not have a priestly class (4) entrusted with the task of ministering to the faithful. It does not have a doctrine of special revelation from the other side (5). Finally, it does not have a sacred literature (6). However, there *is* an area where traditional religions and humanism overlap. Both are concerned with morality.

7. All of the monotheistic religions propound a way of life and a moral code. Foremost are the rules governing the duties of the religious life. The highest duty of man is to love and fear the Lord and his commandments. This includes the commandment to observe the Sabbath and to follow prescribed prayers, ceremonies, and rituals. Waves of religious reformers such as Jesus have disputed a literal interpretation of many laws, proclaiming that it is the spirit and not the letter that we should follow. In any case, an essential component of religious morality is man's duty not only to God but also to his fellow human beings.

All religions lay down guidelines governing human relationships. The Old Testament commands us to obey the numerous rules and regulations enunciated in the Mosaic law. The Muslim is enjoined to follow the Koranic code. Jesus bid us to "love one another."

The religions of Asia likewise are deeply concerned with moral instruction. Although there are wide variations in these religions, many of them focus on self-centeredness. "Their goal is always release from suffering, *my* suffering, as well as the suffering of humanity."[11] In Western secular philosophies, the goal of happiness is the intelligent satisfaction of desire. For many Asian religions the suppression and renunciation of desire point the way to spiritual growth and enlightenment. To be able to transform desires is held to be the "higher," "inner," or "deeper" level of consciousness.

Although there are different paths to virtue, the point is that religions seek to chart the way. In some, there are extremely detailed formulas. They govern everything from sexual morality, procreation, the relationship between the sexes, and marriage to the duties of children to parents and vice versa, of friends to friends, of subjects to rulers, and of everyone to strangers within their midst. They may include prohibition of some foods (for example, pork or any meat), the rite of circumcision, and rules governing a wide range of economic and social relationships. All of this is in the range of normative value judgments, for certain things are considered good or bad, right or wrong; the religious code outlines acceptable modes of conduct—allegedly derived from God.

In these systems it is difficult for the ordinary person to achieve the highest state of spiritual bliss. Hindu holy men, Buddhist monks, and Christian saints have to cultivate the arduous task of spiritual self-development. It is uncertain how many have actually achieved the Zen Buddhist's *satori* state of illumination or the saint's mystical union with God. Many believers find such a spiritual quest too rigorous to pursue; still they can observe religious righteousness.

If a philosophy or eupraxsophy focuses primarily on ethics or morality, is it a religion? I think not. For although humanism, skepticism, Stoicism, Epicureanism, Marxism, existentialism, and pragmatism all have something concrete to say about normative values and although many recommend a way of life, the very fact that their ethical judgments are analogous to those of traditional religions does not make them religions.

An interesting question, indeed, is whether the terms *religion* and *philosophy* can even be applied to all the varieties of "religion" we encounter in the world. Buddhism, Hinduism, Taoism, and Confucianism do not fit Western conceptions of religion. Asian systems are unique and there are so many divergences that even the term *philosophy* may not apply to them, even though Western writers have attempted to stretch the terms *religion* and *philosophy* to cover them.

CONFUCIANISM

Is Confucianism an ethical system or is it a religion? In Confucianism, the supernatural and the sacred recede into the background, and a life stance with an emphasis on practical or prudential choice begins to prevail. No doubt there are religious elements in Confucianism—the worship of one's ancestors, for example. But Confucianism seems at the far end of a scale of religion, for it emphasizes moral virtue rather than sacred duties, ritual, and prayer.

Confucianism generally dominated Chinese civilization for twenty-five hundred years. Confucius (K'ung Fu-tzu, 551–479 B.C.) was born in the province of Lu. He was married at an early age, served as a government official, and was very successful as a teacher. He advocated social reform largely by educating people to follow ethical rules of conduct. His central moral principle was *jen*, which referred to sympathy, love, benevolence, humanity, and reciprocity. *Jen* was defined as "perfect virtue," transcending the limits of race, creed, or time. In his work, *The Analects*, two important concepts are spelled out: *hsiao*, which refers to filial piety, and *ti*, fraternal love. Both ideas express unselfish, human attitudes. The basic structure of higher Chinese society rested on *hsiao* and *ti*, the obligations and duties owed to parents and relatives. In *The Analects* two further concepts are presented: *chung*, (faithfulness) and *shu* (altruism). The former refers to being completely honest with oneself, the latter to sympathy and understanding with the outside world. The concept of *jen* (loving others) refers to true and unselfish love, singleness of mind. Confucius places great emphasis on the search for knowledge. Confucius said in *The Analects*: "Failure to cultivate virtue, to perfect my knowledge, to change while I hear what is right and to correct my faults—these are the thoughts that worry me." He refused to speculate about the nature of the gods since they are unknowable.

The Confucian system was developed by later writers. Mencius, born about a century after the death of Confucius, developed the concept of *yi*, which refers to the appropriateness of an action within a situation and our obligation to carry it out, instead of to an action done solely for profit. Mencius wished to couple *jen* (what we hold in our hearts) and *yi* (the proper way of guiding conduct). The doctrine of the mean or balance would govern *yi*. Another champion of the Confucian ethical code was Hsün Tzu, who emphasized *li*, a code of ritual politeness and etiquette; this perhaps involved a religious component but applied more to governing rituals within the group, which served as norms for conduct. For this reason, Confucianism is a eupraxia, a normative code of conduct, perhaps even a philosophy of living. It is fairly humanistic in its ethics, with little or no supernatural element.

Confucius's teachings can be interpreted as a purely naturalistic school of morality similar to Aristotle's. Confucius was a sage who offered wisdom in conduct. Some writers have sought to interpret Confucianism as a religion since filial piety involves not only obligations to living parents but also to dead ancestors, with veneration and prayer to honor them. Some have even gone further to venerate and deify Confucius. But when we refer to our earlier definition of religion, we note that Confucianism has no supernatural concept of the sacred or ideas about salvation and a future life. When Confucius was questioned about the realm beyond life he replied emphatically, "If you are not able to serve men, how can you worship the gods?"[12]

Nevertheless an integral part of Confucianism—derived, I might add, from traditional cultural practices that Confucius accepted—was ancestor worship, with attendant ceremonies and sacrifices, which later developed a degree of superstition and mythology. However, Confucius introduced no church or priesthood, nor did he sanctify or glorify God. Instead, the focus was on the family and rituals within it. And there was no doctrine of salvation. Although the Confucians were grateful for whatever Heaven might give them, in the last analysis the Confucian code has a profound respect for life and an ancillary notion of happiness. A devotee of Confucius must depend on his own virtue to achieve happiness, not on external circumstances or divine beneficence. Human relationships are emphasized and men and women are taught how to live in harmony and balance with each other in the spirit of fairness, justice, tolerance, and compromise. A person has duties to himself, his family, his community, his nation, and the world. It is within the family, at least, that loyalty (*chung*) and altruism (*shu*) were nobly expressed.

What is perhaps absent from Confucianism is *sophia* in the broader sense, for there is no highly developed, cosmic world view in the metaphysical or scientific sense, nor is there an emphasis on objective experience or rationality as a way of testing one's knowledge of the world.

My definition of religion applies especially to Christianity, Judaism, and Islam, the three great monotheistic religions; and it also applies to innumerable sects, denominations, and cults that have sprung up. But does this definition apply to other Asian religions? Any delineation of Asian religions must be ragged around the edges; for the way they developed has depended upon unique historical, cultural, and political forces at work in the areas in which they flourished.

HINDUISM

What about Hinduism? Surely this religion satisfies our definition. The term *Hindu* originally meant "Indian" and referred to the beliefs and practices of innumerable generations of people living in or near the Indian subcontinent. Hinduism has spanned some 5,000 years. It is a very diversified tradition with great variety and different streams. It has been influenced by other religious traditions, including Buddhism, Christianity, and Islam; and its influence has spread and been felt throughout the world.

The Hindi scriptures include the *Vedas*, texts written over the course of 1,500 to 2,000 years before the Christian era. These include the *Rig Veda*, a collection of hymns addressed to the gods that were introduced by the Aryan invaders of Indian soil. Among the hymns are those dedicated to Indra, the god of storm and war; to Varuna, universal ruler of the law; and to Agni, the god of fire. There are prose texts, such as the *Brahmanas*, which deal with sacrificial rituals; philosophical texts, such as the *Upanishads*, and many other authoritative texts. Some use the term *Veda* for the earliest texts and *Vedanta* for the later texts, which are more philosophical. The *Bhagavad Gita* (Song of the Lord), more than any other text, has provided guidelines for Hindu thought and conduct.

Two components of our definition of religion are clearly present in Hinduism: (1) There is a sense of the sacred, of some ultimate transcendent realm. The idea of absolute Brahma points in the direction of a pantheistic monism. The mystic seer or holy man can begin to discover the divine dimensions of reality, beyond desire and pleasure, achievable by renunciation. (2) There is thus a belief in spiritual paths to peace and salvation. Hinduism has a belief in the transmigration of souls. The present span of life is only one in a succession of lives. What a man or woman is today is determined by what he or she has done in previous lives. *Karma*, or moral causation, plays a role, particularly if one can achieve *moksha*, emancipation from the limits of present existence. To achieve this state, it is necessary to transcend ignorance (*avidya*) and illusion (*maya*).

Thus Hinduism affirms the promise of the spiritual and addresses the need for self-discipline (*yoga*) in order to obtain release from the cares of the world. Presumably, the end-path to salvation is to achieve a kind of union with Brahma, the ultimate reality transcending all categories of thought or ordinary experience, the "supreme divine spirit" pervading the universe, the origin of all, the source of all understanding. The concept of *Atman,* or great self, is at the heart of absolute reality. Although the Hindus have no idea of personal immortality, nor of theism as in Western monotheism, a spiritual depth pervades their religion and philosophy. Following from the idea of spiritual quest is an elaborate system of rituals, a moral code governing a way of life, and holy men to interpret it. Moreover, there developed a caste system and a way of life that pervaded Indian culture and was sanctified by religious practices. Worship also plays an important role, and there are any number of gods and their various incarnations, such as Krishna, Siva, and Vishnu, who are venerated. There is little question that the term *religion* applies to Hinduism.

Scientific humanists are highly critical of Hinduism, with its claims of a hidden reality and a prescientific mystical-metaphysical effort to unravel that reality. Moreover, the moral quest for spiritual peace, at least for the Promethean, seems like a futile effort to escape from this world and its challenges. Its social polity appears to be the effort of an impoverished society to maintain a stable social order, in which the lower classes are kept in their place by spiritual opium and a quest for ultimate release. In any case, whatever its virtues and limitations, Hinduism surely satisfies our definition of a religion.

BUDDHISM

It is difficult to classify Buddhism in all its forms as a religion. Many or most expressions of Buddhism are religious, but there are some notable exceptions to that designation.

The term *Buddhism* derives its name from the Buddha, literally "the enlightened one." Although his personal life is overlaid by legend, we know that Siddhartha Gautama was born of a wealthy and noble family near Benares, in northern India, about

563 B.C., and he died about 483 B.C.E. He married, sired a son, and was being prepared for a life of power and luxury by his father. But at the age of 29, he became aware of human suffering and the limitations of existence. He renounced his worldly possessions and became a wanderer and a hermit. After six years of seeking, he underwent a period of intense illumination and rapture while sitting under a *bo* (fig) tree. Thereafter, he devoted his life to teaching what he had discovered. He attracted disciples who became monks, seeking to follow his way in order to obtain enlightenment also.

Buddha taught that this life is full of sorrow and disease, decrepitude and death, that the highest good is to be released from the goadings of desire and to achieve a state of nirvana, or non-being. He was impressed by the impermanence of all things and the ephemeral character of human existence, and he wished ultimately to be emancipated from struggle and stress. This is difficult to achieve because each person is a part of the great chain of being, composed of parts that have always been united; they are separated by death, but they are reunited again in the future. Buddhism accepts the doctrine of reincarnation and the transmigration of souls. It is only by the exercise of karma that one can eventually be released from sorrow and obtain a state of nirvana. There are various stages that a Buddhist must go through in the hope of reaching this highest stage. The "four noble truths" were discovered by Buddha during his enlightenment. *Dukkha*, or suffering, is endemic to human existence. It has its roots in selfish cravings. The way to achieve peace is to overcome selfish desires by following a "noble eight-fold path," composed of right knowledge, right aspirations (avoid sensual pleasure; do not hurt any living creature), right speech, right behavior, right livelihood, right effort, right mindfulness, and right absorption. The focus was on self-denial, gentleness, and compassion for others.

Buddha was not an ascetic but advocated moderation and the "middle way."

One cannot find a doctrine of the supernatural in Buddhism, at least as understood in Western religion. There is no conception of God as a person, no cosmic plan, no idea of personal immortality or salvation. In the traditional sense, Buddha was an atheist, for he rejected theism. There is, however, another meaning of the godhead, a transcendental reality in which All is One. Nirvana is not God, yet reality ultimately is incomprehensible, indescribable, and only pierced by the mystic's eye of illumination. In this sense, there is a transcendent, divine, or sacred character to the universe, as it applies to the totality of being. This lies behind the world of matter and flux and is due proper veneration and awe.

Buddha did not claim to be a god, nor did he transmit any specific revelations from a god on high. After his death, his beliefs and practices were transformed into a religion by others—though like Christianity Buddhism is split into differing sects. The two main branches are Theravada and Mahayana Buddhism, each more or less dominant in different geographical regions. Theravada Buddhism centers on man as an individual and his quest for personal release, and the adherent is not dependent upon the salvation of others. Mahayana Buddhism ties the fate of each individual to the fate of all. Theravada holds that the man is on his own in the universe and that each person should develop self-reliance. It has developed an elaborate system of monasteries, where Buddhist monks strive for renunciation of worldly desires in an effort to achieve the highest truths. Mahayana Buddhism, by contrast, is a religion for ordinary persons, who have an obligation to serve others. The Theravada monk emphasizes private meditation. Mahayana believers add supplication, prayer, and ritual, calling upon the Buddha for help. For some, Buddha became almost a savior. Some forms of Buddhism borrowed from the indigenous religions of South and East Asia and have developed deities to venerate. Such forms begin to approach Western religions.

Our discussion of Buddhism shows that it is difficult to find a common unitary thread underlying all religions; for some forms of Buddhism, such as Zen (which spread to Japan from China and developed there), the emphasis is on personal self-realization and enlightenment. Buddhism thus expresses a kind of eupraxia or life stance, focusing as it does on right conduct as the source of peace. It seeks to cultivate a style of life in order to achieve a state of release. Some Western thinkers have been attracted to Buddhism insofar as it is devoid of the mythology of a supernatural, miraculous religion and the doctrine of salvation by grace, but especially since it focuses on achieving moral equanimity in this life.

FUNCTIONAL DEFINITIONS OF RELIGION

Each of the classical religions has a central moral theme. Each draws upon a sacred tradition to sanctify the codes of conduct it cherishes. Each lays down moral commandments and obligatory rules that are considered to be divinely inspired. I have argued in *Forbidden Fruit* that the moral code in many cases precedes the religious faith and that religion is used after the fact to sanctify it. Although claiming to be divine, all such religions are creations of the human imagination.

The classical religions also prescribe a social polity, seeking to apply their moral doctrines to society. Devout true believers cannot rest content unless they try to extend their religious faith to the entire fabric of social life. In Islam there is no separation of church and state, and religious law pervades all sectors of a Muslim society. Judaism, before the Diaspora, expressed the national identity of a people, giving a divine support for the social-political structure. For a long time, Christianity and the Bible were enforced by the sword; it was imposed by secular rulers on the subjects living within their realms—from the

Roman emperor Constantine to later European monarchs. The state was used to suppress heresy and enforce obedience to Christian faith and virtue.

It was only with the democratic revolutions of modern times and the conflicts between secular rulers and church authorities that the principle of separation of church and state was enunciated; dissenters were now protected from the power of church orthodoxy. The saving grace of such religiosity was the insistence that conscience was a private matter—though there are continuing efforts by diehards to impose religion on the public square.

Religion thus has had both moral and social functions. Is this what is essential in defining religion? And should we not consider humanism to be a religion, precisely because it shares with traditional religions these two functions? I have denied that; for I submit that religions have usurped their roles when they intrude themselves into the moral life and the political arena and insist that a particular religion should have a monopoly over moral and political decisions. The need to defend moral and political freedom from repressive theological doctrines is now widely recognized as essential to the cause of human liberty.

Religions surely have the same rights as eupraxsophies; they are entitled to express their genuine moral concerns for human welfare. Indeed, a moral passion for righteousness in one sense is the driving foundational interest of all other human concerns. The problem arises when a religion claims to have an exclusive corner on morality, insists that morality is inextricably tied to the supernatural, and asserts that no other moral claims independent of its divinely ordained commandments are legitimate. The same misgivings are applicable to those theologies which are converted into theocracies and strive to dominate political power in the name of God.

The fallacy of identifying religion with a moral code or a social polity can be seen in other areas as well. Religions have also competed with science, philosophy, and education historically; they have sought to impose their metaphysical theories of the universe; they have censored dissenting scientific and philosophical opinion and indoctrinated schoolchildren. We recognize today that science should not be entangled with religion and that freedom of research needs to be defended—as the trials of Giordano Bruno and Galileo and the battle of creationists against evolution vividly testify. Similarly, philosophy is a field of study pursuing its own goals and using its own methods of rational inquiry quite independent of theology. Neo-Thomists, such as Jacques Maritain, thought that theology and philosophy were separate disciplines, each having a kind of autonomy, but that the conclusions of natural and revealed theology would be the same. One cannot interfere in the philosophical quest, he said, though if a philosopher had reached conclusions contrary to the faith, he was mistaken.[13] Religionists have been keenly interested in the education of the young, and they have attempted to use the schools to instill their religious doctrines. Indeed, religions have attempted to encompass all human interests and dominate the totality of life. The secular revolution of modern times attempted to wrest control of other institutions in society from church domination. Although religions have sought to dominate these other human interests, they have been retrieved by secular and humanist forces. The fact that nonreligious institutions have social or moral functions does not ipso facto make them religious. Implicit in this argument is a basic confusion about the definition of religion.

The essential characteristic of a religion, I have argued, is the division of the universe into the sacred and the secular, with veneration of the former; but this should not be confused with any moral, political, scientific, philosophical, or educational roles that religion has appropriated to itself in the past. Now there are those who will disagree with my definition of religion; they insist that we should not define religion by the *content* of the beliefs but by their *functions*. Using a functional analysis, humanism, they maintain, is a religion, for it exercises roles analogous to those of religion.

The functional approach to religion was given powerful philosophical impetus by Immanuel Kant. In *The Critique of Pure Reason*, Kant demonstrated that one cannot prove three classical propositions of speculative metaphysics: the existence of God, freedom of the will, and immortality of the soul. These concepts lack any experiential content, and they have no identifiable empirical meaning. Kant demonstrated the antimonies that ensue when we attempt by pure formal argument to prove or disprove them. He rejected the famous ontological, cosmological, and teleological arguments for the existence of God. He showed that all such logical proofs are exercises in futility, for one is engaged in a dance of bloodless concepts, devoid of any perceptual content. Kant ended up an agnostic about the central conceptual postulates of theism.

Scientific knowledge, unlike speculative metaphysics or theology, was for Kant well grounded, for it represented a union of concepts and percepts and had both an a priori and synthetic basis. Metaphysics and theology were without any reliable ground because they offered up pure concepts empty of percepts; such abstract ideas about the noumenal world leaped beyond the world of phenomena. Kant's skeptical conclusions about the knowledge of God were intolerable to some minds because they implied that theistic religion had no secure anchor in human experience, but was simply an article of faith. If we can make no reliable cognitive claims to theological truth, is belief in a deity a complete absurdity? Is it so bound up with contradictions that a rational person can no longer accept it? Are we thus forced to abandon any pretensions to religiosity? Kant was himself troubled by the skeptical conclusions that he had reached in the *Critique*, but he found another opening to religious belief: the glimmerings of the noumenal within the recesses of the moral self. Examining the phenomenology of the ethical life, he discovered that we have moral duties and responsibilities. Kant noted, however, that there is an antimony between moral duty and personal happiness and that fulfilling the dictates of the former may mean a sacrifice of the latter. He attempted to reconcile this disparity by postulating God, freedom, and immortality on purely ethical grounds. Although we cannot prove that God will judge the choices made by our free will, the moral life requires these postulates. Justice presupposes that the virtuous will be rewarded and the immoral punished in some ultimate divine accounting. All of this points to other criteria for interpreting the meaning of religious beliefs. It also provides justifying reasons for those who wish to vindicate their right to believe in God. Does it also suggest that one cannot behave responsibly unless he believes in God or that one cannot have a true ethics without God?

These latter claims are mistaken, for it is clear that individuals can and do have a keen sense of their moral obligations and duties without necessarily believing in God. Thus it simply is not the case that the ethical life demands belief in God. The followers of Aristotle, Confucius, and Buddha belie that claim. Indeed, Kant himself argued for the autonomy of practical moral judgment without the need to deduce it from an underlying presupposition. It is clear that many people who believe in God and a divine judgment day are nonetheless immoral, and conversely that even if such a belief is absent, moral agents may behave ethically, abiding by the dictates of the moral conscience. Further, one can have a well-founded ethics in humanism.

Some maintain that it is not the *truth* of a religious claim but its *functional value* that is important. Functionalists have argued that religions should be judged on pragmatic grounds, not by what they say but by what they do. It is the consequences of our beliefs in practice that is the real test of their efficacy. William James introduced this pragmatic argument in his essay *The Will to Believe* in order to justify his belief in a divine universe.[14] We judge religions not by what they say but by the actions of their adherents, i.e., by their effects upon morality and other vital functions.

Shall we accordingly consider a set of propositions religious, not by what they state or imply but by what kind of conduct they lead to? Do humanistic belief systems then share functions with theistic belief systems, and do they thereby qualify as religions?

This raises a deeper epistemological question about the nature of language. It is no doubt true that if you wish to define a term, you must examine how it is used in context. We should not ask for its formal meaning alone but also for its function or use, and we can understand the former only by reference to the latter.

God-language obviously has many functions and uses: it is *imperative*, insofar as sets of ethical commandments flow from it; it is *evocative*, insofar as it expresses deep feelings and emotions; and it is *performative*, insofar as it stimulates ceremonies and rituals. But religious language, I submit, has as a core function the *informative* or *designative* use of language; namely, it points to the existence of some alleged divine or sacred source of reality, some ultimate transcendent being or beings, over and beyond the world of ordinary experience.

The two central issues here concern the *meaning* of religious language and the *justification* of its claims. In my judgment the claim that God exists has not been corroborated, verified, or validated. It is, I submit, untrue by any acceptable meaning of the term *truth*. In more carefully guarded language, I would say that the claim that God exists is improbable and hence most likely false. The burden of proof, in any case, rests with the proponents of such a claim; it is not the primary duty of the skeptic to prove the negative. The inability over the millennia of the theologian to demonstrate or verify the existence of God is the primary reason I am skeptical about it. After all is said and done, the central claim of religion is essentially vacuous, devoid of clear meaning and truth. Religion, as we have understood it, is a projection of human longing, a tale spun out of the web of human interests, a contrivance invented to satisfy human wishes. Nonetheless it involves, at a minimum, the belief in (if not the truth or actuality of) the sacred and our obligation to venerate it.

The study of human culture demonstrates paradoxically that a system of belief does not have to be true to have force and that men and women will die for a holy cause even if it lacks any empirical foundation. This is surely true of virulent religions. It also applies to other belief systems. For example, astrology has persisted for more than five thousand years, despite the failure of scientists to prove its central thesis: that the time and place of birth are related to the planetary-celestial configurations and that these determine our personality and destiny. For the belief that a person's destiny is tied up with the stars is reassuring, it gives a person a place in the universal scheme of things. Is this not all the more so for Judaism, which fervently claims that the Jews are the "chosen people of God"? What suffering they have endured over the millennia to perpetuate this ethnic myth. Similarly for Christianity and Islam, which claim universality in their sweep, and a God who promises eternal salvation. No amount of argument will dissuade a true believer of his first postulate—if he hungers for cosmic reassurance.

Let us explore in greater detail the arguments of the functionalists. Some liberal religionists, many sociologists of religion, and some humanists have argued that even if the term *God* has no empirical or descriptive referent, this does not mean that it is totally devoid of meaning; the belief in God may have moral, aesthetic, sociological, psychological, and existential functions. They have attempted to locate the functional equivalents of God-talk in human psychology and culture, rejecting the claim that it has a cognitive truth-function. The arguments of John Dewey and Paul Tillich are especially relevant here. Both writers have used variations of the functionalist argument. Although Dewey was a thoroughgoing naturalistic humanist who rejected the belief in a supernatural deity and wished to abandon traditional religion, he nevertheless used the term *God*, redefining it to apply to humanism. Tillich, an influential Protestant theologian, wished to retain the classical symbols and metaphors of Christianity, but nonetheless gave them radically altered existential meanings.

DEWEY'S DISTINCTION BETWEEN RELIGION AND THE RELIGIOUS

In his book *A Common Faith*, John Dewey makes an important distinction between *religion*, as an institutionalized system of beliefs and practices and the *religious*, referring to certain qualities of experience. He points out that there are such a multitude of religions that it is difficult to formulate a generic definition that covers all of them. He recognizes that religion has been tied to the supernatural and that theistic religions emphasize the belief that "some unseen higher power" controls our destiny and is "entitled to obedience, reverence, and worship."[15] Dewey says that in this age of modern science it is no longer possible to entertain a belief in a divine being. Nevertheless, there are qualities of experience that he thinks too important to abandon, and he wishes to use the term *religious* to designate these. Here he is not talking about mystical or quasimystical experiences in which someone claims to have a sense of the exalted presence of God. The *religious* does not denote a specific entity; it denotes, rather, "attitudes that may be taken toward every object and every proposed end or ideal."[16] Dewey uses the term religious to refer to those aspects of experience which contribute to the integration of our purposes, to "those ideals and ends so inclusive that they unify the self." In this sense, the *religious* involves morality tinged by emotion. For Dewey, religious faith is a "unification of the self through allegiance to inclusive ideal ends which imagination presents to us . . . as worthy of controlling our desires and choices."[17] Among the ends that naturalists can cherish is faith in the methods of intelligence, democracy, science, and education. Like other religious symbols and beliefs, these ideals can provide some meaning for life and contribute to its integration.

Many liberal religious humanists have applauded Dewey's distinction. If humanism is not a religion in the usual acceptance of that term—as an institutionalized set of beliefs and practices fixated on a deity—at least it expresses many of the qualities of religious experience; that is, there is a devotion to a cause and a commitment to moral ideals that are worthy of human attainment. The humanist, no less than the theist, heroically and passionately espouses his moral ideals, seeks to defend them from their detractors, and devotes his life to their implementation.

In an effort to make pragmatic intelligence and democratic vistas palatable to critics, Dewey chose to use traditional language, though with an altered connotation. He identified elements of morality, dedication, and emotion in the faith of religious believers; and he had sought to show that naturalists and skeptics are capable of similar intensities of moral dedication and heightened feeling.

I am afraid that his reinterpretation, however understandable, has left something out, namely, the central meaning of religiosity. After all, *religious* is an adjective derived from the noun *religion*. According to *Webster's Ninth New Collegiate Dictionary* the term *religious* refers to that which relates to or manifests "faithful devotion to an acknowledged ultimate reality or deity." A religious person is "devoted to religious beliefs or observances" and is "scrupulously and conscientiously faithful." In other words, to say that someone is *religious* means that he "manifests devotion to religion" and that he is "pious" and "godly." Generally, a religious person is one who "lives his religion" or "belongs to a religious order or institution." He is said to "follow his teachings." He is "faithful," "strict," "conscientious," "fervent," and "devout." Not all religious people are churchgoers, yet it is said that there are "inner convictions of the heart," as in the Protestant's approach to God by means of internal soliloquy. Thus a religious person in this sense believes in or knows God inwardly and seeks to follow the divine example in his life. Accordingly, we cannot entirely divorce the *religious* from *religion*, as Dewey attempted to do, without judging their meanings.

Dewey unnecessarily obfuscates the issue by retaining the word *God*. In *A Common Faith*, he explains that "God . . . denotes the unity of all ideal ends arousing us to desire and actions" and represents a "unification of ideal values."[18] He states: "It is this active relation between ideal and actual to which I would give the name 'God.' "[19] Now Dewey surely does not believe in the reality of a divine being. He is an atheist. Yet he does not wish to abandon the term "God" entirely. In not doing so he has unintentionally compromised the ethics of clarity. Two of Dewey's students, Sidney Hook and Corliss Lamont, protested his redefinition of a classical term. Both Hook and Lamont have denied that humanism should be construed as "religious." But Dewey's views had a strong influence on humanists who wished to find some common ground with liberal religion.

Paradoxically, his views have had an unanticipated influence on religious conservatives as well, who maintain that secular humanism is a religion and who quote John Dewey to make their case. They do so in part in order to exclude things they don't like from the public schools—labeling them "secular humanist." For if humanism, even naturalistic and secular humanism, is a religion, then we would be faced with a violation of the First Amendment to the United States Constitution, which states that "Congress shall make no law respecting the establishment of religion or the free exercise thereof." This effort at redefining religion in such a way that not only religious humanism but also secular humanism become religious turns language upside down; like Lewis Carroll's Alice-in-Wonderland, conservatives seek by arbitrary fiat to make words mean whatever they want. Following this definition, atheism, as well as theism, is religious; but then virtually anything and everything may function religiously, and all distinctions collapse. In my judgment Dewey's use of religious language leads to unnecessary obfuscation.

TILLICH'S RELIGION AS "ULTIMATE CONCERN"

This extreme redefinition of *religion* is given added impetus by Paul Tillich. Tillich wishes to reinterpret all religions in humanistic terms. He does not focus on the object of religious veneration—God as a Being—but on the experience of ultimacy itself. According to Tillich, human beings are concerned about many things in life but, in contrast with other amoral organisms, they have "spiritual" aspects. Some of these are both urgent and fundamental. "Faith," he says, "is the state of being ultimately concerned."[20] If a faith claims to be "ultimate," it demands the total surrender of those who accept the claim, and it "promises total fulfillment." An example of this is the faith manifested in the Old Testament. The ultimate concern is with the universal God of justice. Yahweh is "the ultimate concern of every pious Jew." The first and most basic commandment is: "You shall love the Lord your God with all your heart, and with all your soul, and with all your might" (Deut. 6:5). Thus faith "demands total surrender" to the subject of the ultimate concern.

For Paul Tillich the content of the faith-state may vary infinitely. But it does not matter for the formal definition of faith, since there can be different ultimate concerns. For example, a national group may take the life and growth of the nation-state as its ultimate concern; it demands that all other concerns be sacrificed to it. Or again, one can be ultimately concerned with success, social standing, and economic power. Thus achievement and success dominate many people in competitive Western societies and become their god, demanding unconditional surrender and promising fulfillment.

For Tillich, faith as ultimate concern is "an act of a total personality." It lies at the dynamic center of his personal life, involving both unconscious, nonrational, and consciously rational free choice. If there is an unconditional surrender, it involves "ecstasy," including intellect, emotion, and will. For Tillich, the divinity of God is focused on the unconditional and the ultimate. One's ultimate concern unites the subjective and objective aspects of faith. "There is no faith without an interest toward which it is directed." But there is no ultimacy without the subject being likewise involved.

What about traditional religion? Tillich's own ultimate concern included Christianity (as well as religious socialism), but he radically reinterpreted the meaning of its symbols. Symbols point to something beyond themselves; they participate in that to which they point. They allegedly open up to a reality and our soul, which otherwise would be closed to us. They cannot be produced intentionally but express the collective unconscious. Tillich was a student of Rudolf Bultmann (1884–1976), the skeptical German theologian who demythologized the Bible. We know next to nothing about the Jesus of history, said Bultmann, drawing upon the best historical, critical biblical scholarship of his day. Bultmann considered the biblical stories of the Garden of Eden, the fall of Adam, the great flood, the exodus from Egypt, and the miraculous virgin birth, resurrection, and ascension of Jesus as mythological tales that cannot bear the scrutiny of critical scholarship. If Christianity is to retain any meaning, it must be read in metaphorical and symbolic terms, and not in any literal sense. Yet Tillich retains faith, as ultimate concern, in God, beyond any particular God, as the fountain of Being itself. God expresses our ultimate "unconditioned transcendence."

Some critics have found Tillich's language to be clothed in

unnecessary poetic obscurity, stuttered incoherence, and impenetrable fog. In one sense Tillich was an atheist, for he rejects the traditional views of God as a person and of Jesus as the divine Son of God. Yet he uses the language of Christianity to dramatize man's existential plight facing the polarities encountered in Being, and he affirms "the courage to be" in the face of nonbeing, or death.

How are we to evaluate the adequacy of Tillich's theory of ultimate concern? Are some ultimate concerns more genuine than others? Tillich does consider some concerns to be "idolatrous." How are we to recognize fraudulent symbols? He says that the promises they make are not fulfilled and that in the long run they disintegrate rather than integrate the personality. Moreover, he states emphatically that some ultimate concerns are demonic: they have been expressed by Nazism, Stalinism, the Holy Inquisition, and forms of Fundamentalism. Even monotheism can become idolatrous; God can become an idol like the animal gods or half-animal gods of Egypt. In modern discussions of his theory, Tillich has labeled secularized ultimate concerns as "quasi-religions," rather than religions. He also confesses that he is strongly attached to the liberal humanistic tradition.

It is difficult to know how to appraise Tillich's theory of religious symbolism. Is it that which points to the ultimate Being beyond being? Or is it something else? Presumably, one can judge religion not simply by the truth claims but also by other existential functions. Brilliant as Tillich's insights sometimes may be, there is something disingenuous about his willingness to use the language of ancient Christianity, yet to so reinvest it with new meanings that it loses its original force. Why not simply refuse to pour new wine into the same old bottles? Why not take entirely new directions? The failure to do so is no doubt due to trepidation at making a radical rupture with ancient mythologies and fear of declaring an end to the domination of human civilization by the ancient symbols of faith.

I respond that we should not obfuscate language by trying to force new concepts into old words. We should face reality according to our understanding of science. We should establish a new humanistic eupraxsophy with new concepts and the honest use of language. Theologians may well fear to declare an end to the domination of human civilization by the ancient symbols of faith. Why should we be inveigled by their trepidations?

FUNCTIONALISM REAPPRAISED

It is time that we evaluate afresh the functions which religion can serve.

For the functionalist, theistic symbols of belief do not make any descriptive claims in any literal way but are to be read as poetic metaphors. They do not make specific truth claims. Examples would be statements that Jesus was the son of God or that he was resurrected, that Moses transmitted the Ten Commandments from God to the children of Israel, or that Muhammad's proclamations were divinely revealed.

Symbols and beliefs do not allude to the existence of God as a real person or being. God-talk only indirectly refers to Being in general, that is, to the power and structures of the cosmic order that lie beyond our control.

Religious language does not empirically assert that the discarnate personality will survive the death of the body and enjoy eternal life in some new form. It only dramatizes the finitude of human existence, our mortality, and the eventual return of each human to the cosmic ocean whence he emerged.

Religious poetic metaphors do not promise eternal salvation for those who believe as distinct from those who do not. They only provide some existential solace in the face of adversity, and they bolster the courage to persist in spite of death. They only dramatize the brute reality of human finitude.

The functionalist maintains that the religious beliefs and symbols of both theists and humanists have analogous functions. It is not what the beliefs say, they allege, but what they do in human experience and culture that counts. What are the distinctively religious functions of such beliefs? What is unique to *homo religioso*?

1. A system of beliefs—whether theistic or humanistic—that is uniquely religious, according to the functionalists, provides some meaning and direction to life, some overall purpose and guidance. It gathers together the fragmented pieces of our experience and knowledge and provides some integrated unity to them, enabling us to function better. Such a system of beliefs thus has some *psychological role within the internalized self.* The unification of our values and attitudes, they claim, can help us overcome indecision about our place in the universe, and it can help us live better without being mired in skeptical doubts.

2. A religious system of belief may also provide a basis for *moral conduct.* It offers some rationale for self-control and self-direction, the moderation of our inclinations and desires. Moral systems also govern our relations to others. They make us aware of our duties; they enjoin us not to harm other persons, to reduce suffering, to be empathetic and considerate of the needs of all sentient beings.

3. Religious symbols have *sociological functions* in that they provide a common framework of traditions passed down from generation to generation; they become an indelible part of the social fabric. Religious institutions thus ensure some stability in the social fabric. They define—however they may vary–acceptable parameters of moral conduct. They enable us to transmit to future members of the group a revered heritage and thus to guard against conflict. They provide a basis for identity and loyalty as part of a cultural tradition. Insofar as we can celebrate and consecrate the rites of passage and share our sorrows and joys with our tribal community, some social support is provided for the

common crises encountered in living. In drawing on the heritage of the distant past, we can avoid excesses in the present and the future and provide sustenance for solitary individuals who otherwise would have to face the awesome decisions of life alone. Religion thus binds us to our ethnic group; it is one of the emotional bonds between grandparents, parents, and children that defines the person, like his language and culture.

4. A religious system can be a source of *aesthetic inspiration*; it can dramatize the visions and aspirations of a people. It can pour forth in imagery and metaphor the expressions of a cosmic set of ideals, enhanced by the sense of beauty. The arts, architecture, music, and literature can thus be stimulated to new heights of metaphoric expression.

5. Last, but surely not the least, according to the fundamentalists, religion has an ultimate *existential* function. It celebrates birth, the rites of puberty, victory and defeat, marriage and death— all of the key passages in human life. It thus enables us to deal with tragedy; it seeks to provide soothing balm for the shock of death; it provides a system for evoking catharsis. By placing human life within a broader framework, it can relieve us of metaphysical dread of the unknown. In relating the life of each person to the cosmic scene, it can provide us with consolation and hope.

I have enumerated these five central functions of religious belief systems. There may very well be others. But when one looks at those above, one can see that it is not the content of the religious metaphors that are important—they will vary as cultures vary—but the enduring character of the symbols in providing "spiritual" nourishment for our deepest psychological hunger as we seek to plumb the mysteries of eternity. Although the functions have an aura of truth to them, at the same time they generate quandaries for a critical intelligence unable to swallow the religious metaphors whole. If a function satisfies a need, basic or derived, we may ask whether this can be satisfied by nonreligious forms of social life—philosophic, scientific, economic, political, ethical, artistic, or eupraxsophic? To label all of the basic functional needs of humanity as religious is to beg the question and to fixate humanity on earlier prephilosophical and prescientific stages of historical development. I submit that the *content* of a belief system cannot be ignored; its claim to truth is *essential* in evaluating its functional value.

I agree that the preceding list of functions represents the invariant and recurring needs of the human species and that these are not limited to a specific, temporal cultural slab of history. Let me suggest, however, that it is a mistake to say that religious systems of belief and practices are uniquely able to satisfy those needs and/or that any alternative institutional arrangement that seeks to satisfy them is ipso facto to be designated as a religion. A theistic belief system leads to certain concrete forms of practice, and these differ remarkably from a naturalistic belief system. These different kinds of systems cannot be equated. For religious people will engage in prayer and ritual, and nonreligious people will not. A radical change in human culture has occurred because human understanding has developed. Science and technology have augmented our ability to understand nature so that an "occult" explanation is no longer needed. In addition, our sense of power and control over destiny is expanded. Accordingly there is no need to assuage divine powers by prayer. The only point to prayer is evocative: it pours forth our sorrow, expresses our hopes, perhaps even vents our spleen. It has no causal efficacy beyond that.

Supernatural religions postulate "hidden and unseen powers" responsible for what happens to humans on earth, and they delineate our obligations and duties of reverence toward them. Let us disentangle definition from function and content from form in order to see how different belief systems lead to different forms of conduct. It is clear that the functional and behavioral consequences are *not* the same.

Believers in supernatural religions will lead lifestyles different from nonreligious people. Monotheistic believers hold that they are part of a preordained scheme, that what they do is known to and observed by a divine Mind, that God ultimately is responsible for all of creation, and that by altering our beliefs and practices we can influence God's plan. This requires that we have an abiding faith and are obedient to his commandments.

Humanists, in their "ultimate concerns," have no such expectation. They consider the universe indifferent to their wishes and desires. They do not engage in prayer or worship. They have no expectation of a future life. Whatever will be depends not on God's will or on fate, but on luck, chance, and their own efforts. Thus, "ultimate concerns" are not equivalent in their outcomes or functions. Indeed, various systems of belief may have *negative outcomes* or *dysfunctions* when compared with other aspects of behavior. What are some of these?

1. First and foremost is their *effect on truth*. There are different methods for establishing truth claims. Supernatural belief systems are at variance with the scientific view that knowledge claim must be corroborated objectively by reference to evidence and reason before they can be accepted. Religions present myths as true, even though there is little or no evidence to support them. These are based on revelations, miracles, or mysticism. In some cases myths play such a commanding role that devout theists seek to censor those who hold contrary dissenting views, thereby attempting to suppress "heresy." Such systems are out of touch with reality; if held with intensity they can become pathological. If encrusted they become absolutes; as such, they can thwart scientific and philosophical inquiry and limit the creative horizons of human discovery.

2. Where a mythic system is firmly entrenched it can *block ethical progress*. The absolutes of the past are laid down in concrete for the future. Prohibitions, taboos, and phobias dominate; attitudes about divorce, birth control, the eating of certain foods, the role of women, and so forth are taken as strict commandments, binding on the disciples of the True Faith. Any change in

the moral code is viewed with horror. Yet as society changes, there is need to engage in critical ethical inquiry, to modify ancient practices, and to institute new principles and values to guide our conduct. The difference is between morality based upon faith and ethical choice based on rationality.

3. Intransigent moral attitudes may lead to *repressive views of sexuality*. They may condemn as evil all but narrowly defined modes of sexual expression, as for example, all forms of adultery, masturbation, pornography, homosexuality, and premarital relations. Religions often arouse guilt and a sense of sin. Eroticphobia engenders self-hatred and fear, a sense that sex is wicked and has to be obtained or endured, but not enjoyed.

4. On the positive side, a theistic system may lead to humanitarian deeds and a charitable concern for humanity. Negatively, it can be *intolerant of other faith systems*, intransigent and suspicious of diversity and differences. It can engender hateful, mistrustful, fratricidal conflict—all in the name of the true faith. It may lead to ethnic and religious warfare. Inquisitions and crusades were launched by true believers to force their beliefs on others.

5. At its best, the religious impulse may arouse compassion for the underdog and promote cooperative action for ameliorating the human condition. However, religion may seek to *prevent social progress*; fearful of change, it may suppress novelty. Its sociological function, to maintain a stable social order, may become oppressive to those who yearn for freedom, strive for equality, wish to liberate the dispossessed, or extend rights and freedoms to the underclasses of society. Although liberation theology accepts the social gospel, different theological tendencies may impede it. In locating ultimate salvation in the next world, most theology deflects primary concern from ameliorating conditions in this one.

6. Religious systems may inspire works of art—beautiful and eloquent—but they may also be *aesthetically boring, even distasteful and ugly*. Other forms of artistic expression express

facets of the human imagination that break with classical models and focus on a new renaissance and the secularization of human interests and values.

7. Theistic systems of belief, even if mythological, may give solace and comfort to those who seek meaning in life. But they may also *generate profound apprehension of the unknown*, fear of God's punishment, irrational forebodings about occult and demonic forces. They may generate internal repression in the name of absolute piety.

The central questions as I see them are the existential ones: Does theism help us to unravel the mysteries of life? Does it help us to face death? Does it contribute to a better life than humanist eupraxsophies? Other pivotal questions are often raised: Would life have meaning for humans if they knew that God was dead and that the universe had no design or purpose? Is the message of secular humanism too stark to be digested? Do we need the solace of myths to help sustain ourselves? Unfortunately, I do not have any simple response to these queries. The dogged persistence of systems of mythic illusion long after they have been refuted by reason and science suggests very strongly that there lurks deep within the human breast a "transcendental temptation," and that it is not easy to find adequate naturalistic substitutes to satisfy this temptation. Not only are we confronted daily with the lumbering remains of the ancient orthodox religions but, surprisingly, where the old-time religions have been weakened, new cults have often emerged, propagating fanciful new transcendental myths. In Western societies these often assume paranormal or occult forms, and where Western religions are in decline, the mystery religions of the Orient may appear.

In *The Transcendental Temptation* I raised the question of whether there is something sociobiological or even genetic—a "transcendental gene"—which predisposes members of the human species to devise or seek out transcendental myths. Given the strong persistence of such myths in most cultures, one might conclude that there is indeed a deep need within the human species, that we crave transcendental moorings for our finite existence, and that we continually are prone to place our hopes in mysterious unseen powers as the means to salvation.

My main disclaimer for this hypothesis is the fact that transcendental myths are not everywhere present in every culture in the same way. Think of the hundreds of millions of people who have not worshiped a God. For example, China has experienced for more than two millennia the Confucian ethical system, which is not a supernatural religion. Similarly, several Marxist societies have persisted without strong theistic religions, even though vulgarized forms of Marxism attempted to replace them with a secular ideological fervor. In the religious cultures of the Western world, there are significant minorities of secularists and humanists who live full fives without the need of the myths of consolation. Thus the fact that such transcendental belief systems have been absent in significant minorities suggests that the transcendental temptation can be overcome. The real question is *how*.

Undeniably the central function of religion is its attempt to blend individual human purposes into a broader cosmic context, providing an ultimate ontological anchor. Religion constructs a social support system that enables lonely souls to share their values and dreams. In huddling together human beings attempt to fare the winds of adversity and misfortune; and in celebrating together they seek to share the manifest joys that life may bring. By singing hymns of salvation, some men and women apparently feel better able to cope with life's sometimes cruel turns, and they may find consolation in the fanciful tales and parables spun out by religions. Theistic religions project our existential needs; they concoct fantasies to cope with finitude and death. But a crucial question is: Are they *true*? If one doubts this, one must look to an alternative that seems nearer the truth, namely, humanism.

But can humanism provide an authentic solutions to our existential condition? This is the decisive question. If it is to do so, then it needs to set forth on its banquet table cosmic moral poetry that will entice and stimulate us. It must present inspiring new messages that can compete with the shattered myths of yesteryear.

NOTES

1. G. E. Moore, *Principia Ethica* (Cambridge, 1903).

2. Cicero, *De Natura Deorum*, ii, 28, p. 72.

3. Lactantius, *Divinae Institutions*, IV, p. 28.

4. Servius, in a commentary on Vero's *Aeneid*, p. 349.

5. St. Augustine, *Retractationes*, 1, p. 13.

6. E. E. Taylor, *Primitive Culture*, vol. 1, p. 424.

7. James G. Frazer, *The Golden Bough*, 2nd ed., vol. 1, p. 63.

8. E. Crawley, *The Tree of Life*, p. 200.

9. Emile Durkheim, *The Elementary Forms of Religious Life* (New York: Collier Books, 1961), p. 62.

10. Anthony F. C. Wallace, *Religion: An Anthropological View* (New York: Random House, 1966), p. 52.

11. Jacob Needleman, *The New Religions* (New York: E. P. Dutton, 1977), p. 10.

12. *The Sacred Books of Confucius and Other Confucian Classics*, ed. and trans. Ch'u Chai and Winberg Chai (Hyde Park, N.Y.: University Books, 1965); *Analects*, XI, 11, p. 10.

13. Jacques Maritain, *An Introduction to Philosophy*, translated by E. I. Watkins (London: Sheed and Ward, Ltd., 1930), chapters 7–8.

14. William James, *The Will to Believe* (Cambridge, Mass.: Harvard University Press, 1979).

15. John Dewey, *A Common Faith* (New Haven, Conn.: Yale University Press, 1934), p. 3.

16. Ibid., p. 10.

17. Ibid., p. 33.

18. Ibid., pp. 42 and 43.

19. Ibid., p. 51.

20. Paul Tillich, *Dynamics of Faith* (New York: Harper and Row, 1957), especially Chapters 1 and 3.

IV. Conviction
and Commitment

Is humanist eupraxsophy able to develop beliefs that can be held with conviction and values that can inspire us? Can it present a reliable cosmic view of the universe and the place of the human species within it? Can it provide some meaningful guidelines for how to live the good life and achieve the just society?

There are many contending approaches to knowledge. On one end of the scale lies extreme skepticism, a state of being unwilling or unable to make judgments or to take a stand about the nature of reality or the best values to pursue in life. Its natural state is neutrality and indecision. On the other end of the scale is dogmatic religion and ideology, fanatically certain about the truth of its claims and seeking to impose them on all. It will harbor no doubts, nor brook any opposition to its articles of faith.

Some forms of scientific and philosophical inquiry veer naturally toward the neutral pole, and not without reason. For it is essential that we be objective in appraising knowledge claims and cautious about those that are as yet untested.

THE ROLE OF SCIENCE

Let us examine the scientific frame of reference first. The scientist qua scientist is committed to a set of methodological criteria which he needs to follow scrupulously if his inquiry is to succeed. The scientist must be open-minded about all questions. He must not allow his bias to color his judgment. He usually begins with a problem or puzzle that arouses him or others within the community of scientific inquirers. There are facts, perhaps anomalies, that need to be described, accounted for, explained. He asks: "What is occurring and why?" He formulates hypotheses and seeks to test them by observing the evidence. He develops theories which need to be internally consistent with other hypotheses that have already been confirmed and are considered more or less reliable. His theories are tested under controlled experimental conditions. He asks: "What is the cause of this strange disease? Can we isolate the virus?" "How do you explain the perturbations observed in the orbit of the planet Neptune? Is there still another planetary body exerting a gravitational influence on it?" "Why should price inflation suddenly occur? What are its causes?"

Each of these questions is asked in a specialized field of knowledge: biology, astronomy, economics. The hypotheses offered as solutions to the queries may be judged objectively only by reference to the evidence, and the scientist must deduce reasons to support them. Presumably other competent authorities inquiring in the same field can examine his grounds and evaluate the adequacy of his hypotheses. The scientist must not allow his bias to intervene. He may have preconceived hunches about what is happening and why, and these may guide his research. But he must not become the overzealous advocate, allowing his speculative theories to color his data. The court of last resort is a body of his peers, who can appraise the data and methods of verification and corroborate whether or not they support his claims.

Granted that scientists are all too human and that they often allow their predilections to get the best of them. Especially when novel theories are introduced, inquirers have had to contend against strong opposition. It may be an uphill battle to convince the scientific establishment that new claims are reliably supported by the evidence. This has been true of many great scientists who devoted years of unending struggle to vindicate their research projects.

Science is a *human* affair, and it depends in the last analysis upon the energy and efforts that human beings are willing to devote to its success. Cultural fashions also shape attitudes within the community and tend to favor one paradigm over another. Still, if science is to succeed in its ongoing quest for reliable knowledge, scientists must be impartial about their hypotheses and in the evaluation of the evidence. The scientist must ask questions about nature, but he must listen carefully without allowing his preferences or personal convictions to influence the facts he records. The methodological rules governing inquiry and research must be fairly applied. Thus, there is an objective ideal that applies to scientific inquiry, one which members of the community of inquirers share: the appeal to clarity, parsimony, evidence, experimental results, and logical consistency. The scientist qua scientist cannot be an advocate or propagandist. He cannot turn the dispassionate quest for truth into a passionate defense of one theory over another. He must be the disinterested spectator, doing his research and allowing his findings to speak for themselves. This does not mean that he is uninterested—he may be intensely aroused by his project—but only that he does not allow his interests to shift the balance of evidence in favor of one hypothesis. He is not a passive bystander; for science demands an active posing of questions, an ingenious thinking up of solutions, and a creative devising of methods to test hunches. He is only passive in observing and recording the data. To say that the scientist must be neutral within his own field means that he is aware of the evidence in favor of the current theories but also knows the gaps in the evidence and the ragged edges still not resolved.

The field of parapsychology is one that immediately comes to mind by way of illustration. Many researchers have invested years of effort to investigate paranormal phenomena, and they have attempted to devise experimental laboratory conditions to test the claims. Some parapsychologists act as true believers, for they are convinced of the reality of extrasensory perception. But there are also committed skeptics, who, in spite of intensive efforts, have not been able to replicate their results or demonstrate the reality of the phenomena. One must, however, continue to look, and here the only appropriate scientific posture is the persistent fair-minded examination of new hypotheses and data. Science depends on honest inquiry, not advocacy pro or con. All of this needs to be reiterated. Science is among the most important of human endeavors, but it can only be furthered by the open mind and the impartial quest for truth.

There are problems with this dispassionate scientific program, however, for as science moves ahead, it becomes enormously complicated and compartmentalized. If one is to succeed in research, one needs to specialize in a subfield and devote intensive efforts to unraveling the intricacies of that discipline. Within the field of expertise the only effective tools to be used are the rigorous criteria of objective inquiry.

Although it is convenient to divide a subject matter into parts, the specialization that develops may be based on arbitrary divisions, for the objects under study may be continuous and nondiscrete. For example, social scientists focus on political, economic, psychological, or sociological processes, drawing upon the literature and the techniques used within their own specialties; but society is an integrated whole, and the divisions of labor need to be synthesized at some time in the future. Medicine deals with the patient as a whole, yet specializations focus on one or more parts—cardiologists on the heart, ophthalmologists on the eyes, orthopedists on the skeletal system. Who will tie the detailed discoveries into integrated theories about how society or a human being functions? Here there is competition between specialists; but we need generalists who can integrate the body of knowledge derived from these separate disciplines into an overall framework.

This becomes all the more important when one recognizes that, although scientists are interested in expanding basic theoretical research, scientific knowledge has some kind of pragmatic application. Economists wish to understand how the economy functions, but they also wish to apply this knowledge normatively—to lower the inflation rate, stimulate production, or cure a recession. Political scientists wish to understand the nature of political behavior—for example, the role of power in human institutions—but this has implications for the policy sciences; for we wish to know so that we can do. Similar considerations apply to natural scientists. Much of the research conducted in the laboratory is done for the technological applications that may result. With rapid scientific advance, new industries are spawned overnight to put new discoveries to concrete uses: biogenetic research and superconductivity, to mention only two recent trends. This being the case, questions of normative value are at the core of science. There is a give and take between theoretical and practical interests. Social needs and interest at any one time direct theoretical research along specified lines. Often funds are expended because of political considerations. Some kinds of scientific research are given strong impetus during wartime. Enormous military expenditures pay for basic research because of its application to new weapons systems. For example, the progress of nuclear physics was accelerated because of the possible military use of the atom bomb. Related to pure research is the role of invention. Scientific technologies are constantly finding applications for new products. Theoretical discoveries in electromagnetics led to the application of electricity to a wide range of products. Discoveries in theoretical nuclear research led to the nuclear-power industry.

Thus questions are raised constantly: What areas ought we to study? Are there some things that we should not seek to know? Some people, for example, have called for restrictions on bio-genetic-engineering research, for they fear that we will open a Pandora's box, whose discoveries an authoritarian regime may be tempted to use; or they worry that we may inadvertently damage the gene pool. If cloning becomes possible, it might lead to positive, as well as negative, results. Many today are fearful of further research into the Strategic Defense Initiative, or Star Wars, as it is popularly called. Such research might be dangerous to the future of humankind on this planet and might accidentally provoke a nuclear winter. There have been calls for the restriction of scientific research into the relationship between IQ and race, because it might be used by racists to deny equal rights to some racial minorities. After all, we know that the Nazis designated some races as "superior" and others as "inferior." Some people are so frightened about the possible misuses of science that the scientist is viewed as a Frankenstein figure. There has been some retreat from earlier confidence in the ability of science to contribute to human progress.

It is thus difficult to conduct pure scientific research anywhere without taking into account the possible uses and abuses of the knowledge gained. Here questions of value are central to the very doing of science. Ought we to engage in free research in every field of interest? Should we in every case apply the knowledge that we have learned? Questions of right and wrong, good and bad thus become highly relevant.

Virtually every prospective advance in science has been met with doubt and fear. In the past there have been constant efforts to thwart free scientific inquiry. Civil libertarians, on the other hand, insist that we should not censor scientific research but should allow free reign to the inquiring mind. Humans wish to augment knowledge both for its own sake and for the possible long-range benefits for humanity. The right to know is one thing; the application of this knowledge is something else. We have a right to object to the misuses of science, especially where there are noxious consequences. Understanding the nature of heat and the combustion of gas led to the invention of the gas oven. Gas ovens can be used to cook food or heat homes, but they can also be used to murder people, as during the Holocaust. Freedom of research does not entail freedom of application. The dynamic factor in social change in the modern world is the application of the methods of science to nature and society. How are we to evaluate the uses of science? What is the relationship of research to practice, knowledge to action, science to eupraxia?

Science has enormously expanded our understanding of the universe. It has converted the unknown into the known. It has unraveled formerly unintelligible mysteries by discovering the causes of natural phenomena. Thus science has contributed to our comprehension of the nature of the cosmos and our place within it. This runs into direct conflict with religious metaphors and a wide range of cultural beliefs of the past that are in need of revision. Regrettably, many intransigent believers find this aspect of science even more threatening than its impact on technology and industry. For it is unsettling to ancient conceptions of man as a discarnate soul capable of immortality and of a universe where divinity is working out an inscrutable plan.

Is the scientist able to resolve questions concerning the application of his discoveries? In technology he can point out possible consequences of various choices. He can calculate the cost-effectiveness of different courses of action, and he can provide alternative technical means to achieve ends, but is the scientist the best-qualified person to make decisions about what is to be done and why? Can he make wise value judgments?

Unfortunately, scientific specialization, so essential to its advance, is often the chief obstacle to interpreting or evaluating the applications of its findings. The problem is that a scientist who is a specialist in one field may not be competent to judge questions that go beyond his field of expertise. Scientists are citizens like everyone else, and they may be no better equipped than the next person to engage in moral deliberations. For ethical wisdom requires skills that he may not possess. When it comes to judging questions concerning the impact of this knowledge on other domains of knowledge, the problems are compounded, for science is fragmented.

Does this not suggest that there is a need to develop over and beyond scientific specialization the *eupraxsophic frame of mind*, one that can interpret and evaluate the findings of the sciences and critically judge their uses? The techniques used in scientific research are not necessarily the same as those used in ethical decision-making. For example, a man or woman may be deeply involved on the frontiers of astronomical research, yet unable to make a wise decision about family, personal life, or his or her role in the university or society.

Eupraxsophy concerns good conduct and wisdom: how we should use the findings of science, not simply how nature operates. The fact that we can do something does not mean that we ought to do it. One cannot simply derive a normative judgment from a description of the world. Here we enter into the field of individual and social action; and here all of the members of the community, particularly in a democratic society, have some stake in what is undertaken.

Problems of choice thus transform cognitive scientific questions into practical discussions. Corporate executives not scientists, political leaders not pure researchers, most often are those who decide what should be produced or which policy ought to be adopted—hopefully after consulting scientific experts about the consequences and costs of alternative means.

Some people have encouraged the development of the policy

sciences—decision-making theory, game theory, value science, even politics and economics—to help in making wise decisions. Undoubtedly, these fields can provide enormously useful tools to facilitate effective choices. But we still have the problem of how to integrate the detailed knowledge derived from specialized fields.

Another serious challenge we face is how to interpret the various sciences and relate them in a cosmic perspective. How do we interrelate the separate sciences into a broader framework? Is it possible to develop a more comprehensive view of humankind, society, life, or nature, a synthesis of the sciences? Heroic figures in the history of thought have attempted to unify the sciences of the day. Sir Isaac Newton's masterly work seemed to integrate the natural and physical sciences at a crucial moment in history. Ignaz Semmelweis's germ theory of disease provided a powerful tool in medical research. Marx offered a comprehensive theory of historical development, Arnold Toynbee a historical account of the rise and fall of civilizations, and Freud an integrating psychoanalytic theory of human motives. Are all of these theories within the domain of science, or are some of them inherently nonfalsifiable?

The need for integrating theories to tie together the disparate and often fragmented elements of our knowledge is clear. At present the rapidity of scientific progress is such that no one mind seems capable of doing so. A chemist can be an expert in his field, yet may believe deeply in Christianity; a computer scientist can engage in transcendental meditation after work; a mathematician may be a mystic.

It is not inconceivable—and indeed it is likely—that the sciences will ultimately develop their own integrating theories. What would be more appropriate than to have testable scientific theories to unify the principles of political and economic theory, or the laws of biology and psychology, with physics and chemistry? It is important that we attempt to find integrative principles, and it is unfortunate that most scientists are reluctant to venture a cosmic perspective. Since such speculation takes them out of their fields of competence, they suffer the risk of being called dilettantes or popularizers.

THE ROLE OF PHILOSOPHY

Historically, it has been the role of philosophy to support general interpretations of the universe. The pre-Socratics sought to uncover the underlying principles of the universe. Plato postulated the theory of ideas. Aristotle developed concepts and categories that helped interpret and unify the sciences of his day. The classical philosophers have each attempted systematic theories of metaphysics: Aquinas, Spinoza, Descartes, Leibniz, Hegel, and Whitehead, among others. Thus philosophy has attempted to develop a *Weltanschauung*, a general perspective of reality. As we have seen, this task is exceedingly difficult because of the sheer complexity and accelerating size of the body of knowledge. Philosophers today are generally reluctant to try to fit so many pieces of the puzzle together, and they even deem philosophy to be merely one specialty among others. They eschew the broader questions, such as the meaning of life or the nature of the cosmos. Philosophy today, unlike science, is primarily an *intellectual* affair. The philosopher is concerned with knowledge on the meta-level. The primary task of analytic philosophy is to achieve clarity, to get rid of ambiguity, to attain clear meaning, to define terms and concepts, to bring to light hidden presuppositions, and to analyze whether they are internally consistent or contradictory. Philosophy thus hones our tools; it deals with questions about foundations. It does not engage in empirical research nor does it seek to substitute philosophical knowledge for knowledge derived in any scientific field. Critical philosophy is concerned with evaluating the concepts of others in separate fields of knowledge: the sciences, religion, the arts, history, politics, ethics. By so doing these philosophers believe they can best help researchers in their progressive quest for knowledge.

William James observed that philosophy in its earliest stages sought to encompass the entire body of the tree of knowledge. As newer intellectual fields developed, separate branches of the tree of knowledge broke away from the main trunk. Thus, in the seventeenth and eighteenth centuries natural philosophy became natural science. In the nineteenth century, chemistry and biology developed as autonomous fields of inquiry. The social sciences, originally part of social philosophy, became separate disciplines. In the late nineteenth century, the philosophy of mind was transformed into psychology and neurobiology; in the twentieth century, logic became an integral part of computer science. It is as if philosophy proposes and science disposes, by breaking away into distinct fields of scientific specialization once empirical solutions seem available. What remains to philosophy is a "residue of questions left unanswered." Many of these perennial questions have never been fully resolved to everyone's satisfaction: What is the nature of ultimate reality? Does free will exist? is man determined? Does God exist? Is the soul immortal? What is truth, beauty, justice? Can we define the good? And then there are new questions thrown into the hopper of unresolved questions of any age, questions that are spun off by the rapid development of the sciences. And so we ask today: Is there intelligent life in the universe? If so, what would this mean to the human species? Does precognition exist? How would it change our perceptions of time? What does neurobiology tell us about the relationship of mind to brain functions? What import does sociobiology have for our understanding of morality? Is moral altruism found in other species? By dealing with such questions, philosophy thus seeks to clarify meanings, to examine implications, to expose contradictions. It tidies up, so to speak, the conceptual framework of others.

Now this surely is a vital role to play. In any university a department of philosophy can have an important function, and students can be intellectually stimulated by reading great philosophical works. But—and this is a large but—what about the original quest for *sophia*? Can philosophy give us wisdom, that is, some kind of general theoretical understanding of the universe and our place within it? Philosophy historically and almost by definition deals in generalities. Is the philosopher still the wise man able to take the cosmic view? Is he aware of the history of thought and culture, on the one hand, yet attuned to the frontiers of research? Is it the fate of the philosopher to man the rearguard, cleaning up the conceptual debris left by past scientific breakthroughs? Is philosophy ever on the cutting edge, advancing beyond the present, helping to get glimpses of exciting new possibilities? The future of humankind depends in part on our creative audacity, whether we dare to dream of new ideas and to bring these visions into reality. Can philosophy help us in the adventuresome, innovative voyage into the unknown? Or is philosophy simply condemned to tidy up after scientific researchers who have already forged ahead and are far out into uncharted realms? Perhaps it is the science-fiction writer who is the true philosophical harbinger of the future—speculating about the possible, which at some future moment may become the actual-Alas, philosophy cannot do this very well, and thus we must move on into the domain of eupraxsophy.

THE ROLE OF EUPRAXSOPHY

Philosophy presumably involves the love of wisdom, and wisdom can mean many things. It involves some comprehension of what is known and some ability to interpret or relate this knowledge into a meaningful whole, and thus achieve *sophia*. The wise man can sum up what is known and synthesize this into a coherent picture. This is the philosopher-at-large dealing with the broader picture; and the philosopher can provide a valuable service—if only he will undertake this task today as he has in the past. But still he is dealing primarily with the love of wisdom, and this is largely an intellectual affair. Ideas are vital to the life of the mind, and intellectuality is among the highest qualities that we can attain. But man is not simply a passive spectator, beholding in contemplation the majestic scheme of things. He is an actor on the stage of life; he is not only a knower but a doer. The nub of the question concerns not the love but the *practice* of wisdom (*eupraxia*). It is the difference between the stance of the scholar and that of the doer, the passive spectator and the active participant. Thus, we ask, how does one apply wisdom to life as lived? How do we enter into the fray? How do we concretely use our knowledge in the process of living? Here we come directly to *eupraxsophy*.

The Greeks had the ideal of contemplative wisdom: the task of the metaphysician was to understand reality in an abstract way and to make nature intelligible. Knowledge was worthwhile for its own sake, to be enjoyed intrinsically. Man was a curious animal; he found great pleasure in learning about the past, discovering new facts, solving puzzles. All of this is granted. But knowledge also has an *instrumental* function, as we have learned from Francis Bacon. Knowledge is power. We wish to know so that we may do. Knowledge is a tool of action. It is not simply an internal set of ideas within someone's mind; it spills out into the real world in the form of behavior. Knowledge is not locked within the brain cells of an isolated individual but is expressed on the cultural scale through language. It involves transactions, not only between the individual and nature but also between culture and nature.

The Greek philosophers were interested in practical wisdom, particularly in ethics and politics. This involved the art of living well in the fight of reason and of wisely governing states and societies. This is normative wisdom, not merely contemplative but moral wisdom. It begins first with clarifying questions about the meaning of *good, bad, right, wrong, justice,* and *injustice,* on the meta-level; but then it goes on, presumably to recommend paths to take. Aristotle offered recipes that the man of practical wisdom should use if he were to be happy. Later, during the Roman era, philosophical schools, such as Epicureanism, Stoicism, and skepticism, provided guidelines on how to live and how to find peace of mind. They were more or less naturalistic efforts to improve life here and now.

The fact that these Hellenistic-Roman schools of ethical wisdom were overthrown by Christianity is one of the great tragedies in human history. Pagan civilization was conquered by a new mystery religion of the East, and naturalistic ethical philosophy was virtually destroyed by a spiritual quest derived from biblical sources. Although impressive efforts were made by theologians, such as Augustine and Aquinas, to use philosophy, the picture they drew was that of a divine universe, in which the supreme duty of man was to know and love God. Religion and theology had conquered philosophy. One reason for the defeat was the fact that Christianity, and later Islam, offered definite faith and commitment, whereas philosophy seemed to provide only indecision and doubt. It has taken Western culture a long time to wrestle free of the stranglehold that successive waves of Christian-Islamic fervor have had on the free mind. It was only during the Renaissance that a new humanistic morality could emerge independently of religion. The humanism of the period was inspired by rediscovering the classics. It attempted to secularize much of life and to substitute a humanistic rather than a spiritual version of reality. Since that time, science has been liberated from a repressive, authoritarian church, and it enabled modern man to examine the book of nature directly, without benefit of clergy.

Let us return to our original question. Can we develop *sophia*—wisdom in practical life where choices are made by individuals and societies on the basis of rational inquiry *and* wisdom in a sense not emphasized by classical philosophy, wisdom as it relates to living (eupraxsophy), that is, theoretical wisdom that is not simply intellectual *but is itself transformed into the practical*? In short, can we develop a cosmic view (*sophia*) that would enable us to live wisely in the world (*eupraxia*)?

In dealing with this task we need to draw upon (1) the methods of scientific inquiry to enable us to understand nature; (2) philosophical analysis in interpreting and integrating scientific knowledge; and (3) ethical philosophy in developing ethical principles and values on the basis of which we can live. We need to tie these strands together into a *philosophy of life*—but more than that, *into a posture of life*, namely, a *eupraxsophy*. Science, philosophy, and ethics can all contribute to this unity, but eupraxsophy involves another element, namely, a *life stance*. It provides us with both a cosmic outlook and a focus or direction within our lifeworld. In this sense, eupraxsophy is not passive knowledge but its active use. Accordingly, eupraxsophy can compete with religion in a way that scientists qua scientists or philosophers qua philosophers are unable to do. Can the philosopher compete with the theologian for the souls of men and women? Can he qua philosopher seek to deconvert true believers and convince them that their conceptions of reality are mistaken? Can the philosopher debate with the fundamentalist Christian, Jehovah's Witness, Mormon, devout Catholic, Orthodox Jew, Muslim, the committed Buddhist or Hindu? Can the philosopher demonstrate how and why he is skeptical and can he offer a positive alternative?

Time and again my colleagues in philosophy say no, that it is not their mission to descend into the marketplace of ideas. Thus they will not debate theologians, Marxists, conservatives, liberals, radicals, or reactionaries. But if not they, then who will do so? Is the role of philosophers to remain in their ivory towers, secluded from the world, analyzing ideas and debating one another, but never seeking to persuade the public? There have been exceptions to this view of the philosophic mission: Marx and Dewey believed that philosophy had a definite role to play in civilization, that it could help transform blind prejudice and habit by means of rational criticism. Nietzsche was an oracle who derided Christianity and socialism and defended the heroic virtues. So did Jean-Paul Sartre, Sidney Hook, and Bertrand Russell. Sartre not only developed a phenomenological existential theory of the human condition but later in life entered into the public political arena. Sidney Hook constantly attempts to use pragmatic intelligence to criticize ideological, religious, and social viewpoints, and he has been forthright in making his views known in the arena of ideas and action. He justifies his beliefs, as did Dewey, on philosophical grounds: philosophers have a role to play in society, and objective judgments about normative matters can be made. Bertrand Russell combined two qualities: He was a skeptical philosopher whose contributions to logic, the theory of meaning, and epistemology were very important; yet he had his own strong convictions upon which he lived and acted. Paradoxically, Russell thought that ethics was not amenable to rational or scientific proof but expressed emotive feelings, for he was aware of the skeptical critiques of the emotionists in ethics. Nevertheless, he was a staunch pacifist who was arrested for breaking the law. He was also throughout his life a resolute defender of sexual freedom, and was fired from the City College of New York for his views. How can we reconcile Russell the philosopher with Russell the activist? He was, I submit, not only a philosopher but a *eupraxsopher* in his public declarations.

By and large, eupraxsophy has not prevailed in the mainstream of the philosophical life, because philosophers deal primarily with *thought*, and to seek to persuade, to the contrary, is to engage in "persuasive definition," perhaps to enter the realm of rhetoric rather than philosophy. Heretofore eupraxsophy has not been enunciated, nor its rationale explained.

If the philosopher qua philosopher will not view philosophy as a way of life, the eupraxsopher will explicitly do so. For the eupraxsopher is not concerned simply with the quest for truth in the world of ideas, as vital as this is to his life, but with life also. In order to live he needs *convictions* upon which he can act and *commitments* to which he can devote his energies. The philosopher may raise objections to any theory—he sees all sides of a question and often cannot make up his mind about any. Philosophy thus never gets beyond the intellectual quest. In this sense, its task is to pose questions, albeit sometimes at the wrong time and in the wrong place. Socrates was a gadfly, and so he was sentenced to death by the Athenians for raising unsettling questions. The philosophic mind deals with questions; it does not provide answers. For even when a solution is proposed, the philosopher sees the difficulties with it and the possible arguments against it. How can the philosopher enter into the fray qua philosopher? Does he not belie his craft as an analytic philosopher? Philosophers lead perilous lives, for when they go outside their craft they can be accused of converting ideas into doctrines, beliefs into dogmas, and betraying their true mission.

RELIGION AND IDEOLOGY

But if the philosopher fears to tread untested waters, others do so with impunity, most especially religionists and ideologues. Let us examine the other end of the scale of human knowledge, religion, where faith is exalted as the preeminent virtue. If we view faith in its extreme sense, it is the willingness to accept as true or real that which is unsupported by evidence or rational proof. Some theologians have exalted the faith-state: "It is the door to things unseen that must first be opened to be understood," declared Augustine. "I believe because it is absurd," asserted Tertullian and Kierkegaard. Belief in Christianity is held to be the most eloquent affirmation of the believer, in spite of obvious contradictions. Although the true believer may find such faith morally worthy, the skeptic deplores the betrayal of the standards of logic and evidence and the self-deception involved. Granted that many religionists wish to use evidence and to be rational to some extent. Modern biblical scholarship has demythologized the Bible, and what survives for some believers is a metaphorical view of God. There are, however, lingering forms of religiosity that persist and involve the willful commitment to doctrines in *spite of evidence to the contrary*.

Such religiosity is an abandonment of all of the standards of objective science and philosophy. Passion dominates critical intelligence. Is not one reason for this sorry state the fact that scientists and philosophers are unwilling or unable to respond to questions or to provide answers to the hunger for meaning? "Does the universe have any purpose?" "What is the meaning of life?" Such questions are rarely answered by the cautious intellectual who will not demean himself to deal with the pleas of ordinary persons. But if the scientist and the philosopher will not respond to these questions, the eupraxsopher will. He has a role to play: for he consciously criticizes the pretentious follies of true believers; he debunks untested tales; and he offers constructive alternatives.

Competing for the souls of men and women in the public arena are ideology and politics, especially the latter, for many have replaced religious faith with a new social dogma, and sometimes even skeptical minds have embraced an ideological-political stance with a vengeance. A good illustration of this, of course, is the devoted Marxist, for whom ideology becomes virtually a holy cause. With the collapse of religious beliefs, new secular messianic ideals fill the void. For many liberal reformers, the chief inspiration for their political views is their indictment of the social order and the desire to transform it into a more just system. Conservatives are likewise determined to defend existing society against its detractors, whom they consider to be immoral. At loggerheads are conflicting moral principles, which are upheld with intense passion by either side, the party of stability versus the party of reform. Stalwart proponents of liberty will view any erosion of it as a threat to the entire moral framework. Some will defend equality, and still others peace, law, and order. A good illustration is the intensity of the abortion debate, where the putative rights of the fetus are pitted against free choice by women.

Political and moral passions may be held as strongly as religious faiths. But often they are held because of class, race, or ethnic background. Here unexamined habits of belief and conduct persist. One may defend a royalist regime because of one's background and breeding; someone else will go to the ramparts because he identifies with the masses. There are free-floating intellectuals who become enthralled with a political ideology; they may even be born-again socialists or libertarians. They may be as firmly committed to their beliefs as those who hold them as mere habit and prejudice.

Such political and ideological beliefs may not be grounded primarily in *cognitive* states; they are inflamed by feelings and emotions. Once a basic belief system is in place, it may be difficult by argument or persuasion to change it; rationalizations can always be made for faults committed by *our* party candidate or cause, which when committed by the other side are considered egregious moral defects.

An American political convention vividly demonstrates the powerful emotive forces at play. These are not unlike Stalin's Red Square on May Day or Hitler's finely tuned and choreographed rallies at Nuremberg, where the crowds were worked into a frenzy during torchlight parades and were overwhelmed by charismatic orators. A candidate for the American presidency similarly may arouse intense feelings. There is excited cheering on his behalf in halls bedecked with flags. Patriotism is the underlying theme. For many their candidate unquestionably has the best policies for the future. The opposing candidate is frowned upon and booed. Such Political antics are like football games, where two teams are pitted against each other and where highly excited crowds egg on the home team and jeer the opponents. Seated on either side are the rooters and the cheerleaders; the sports champions are heroic defenders of the home team.

It is one thing to vent one's feelings in an overflowing sports stadium, where mass psychology holds sway and good clean fun is expressed; it is quite another in the political arena. At the far end of the scale there are ideological belief systems that are based on blind faith in party programs and candidates and that are intolerant of dissent. Certainly such political naiveté warrants criticism. The support of the policies, programs, or candidates of political parties should be chastened by some kind of reflective inquiry. One should recognize that everyone makes mistakes, that policies may have to be modified, and that laws may have to be rescinded in the light of empirical consequences. No one candidate is perfect; no one party has a monopoly on sagacity or virtue. Blind allegiance is no substitute for intelligent political wisdom. Would that we could ground political programs in a study of the facts, a comparative analysis of alternatives, and the testing of their consequences in practice. If any field of human endeavor needs a strong dose of skepticism, it is the political; but a candidate is told that such an attitude will not win voters or enlist voluntary support, and that it would be a dull campaign with no fervor or glamour. But do people need outrageous, simplistic emotional appeals in order to participate in the democratic process? These problems are only compounded by the introduction of television into the selling of candidates.

Similar considerations apply to the economic sphere. The ideal economic model is one in which producers and consumers make intelligent choices based upon cost/price considerations, always calculating self-interest and profit. The rational consumer forgoes expenditures today in order to save for tomorrow, investing his capital in productive enterprises that will provide a return. Under this model, the consumer's choice of products is a function of cost, need, and quality.

Alas, the realities of the marketplace are such that decisions are not based on cognitive considerations alone but on taste, fancy, and caprice. There is a disparity between needs and wants, between rational interests and felt desires; and the passionate feelings of a person will intrude in his cognitive estimations of worth. Advertisers have found that there are subliminal and emotive appeals that will sell their products more effectively than consideration of price or quality. Economic value thus is a function of need-want, cognition-feeling. It involves not simply an intellectual belief-state but attitudinal motivation, the so-called subjective factor that stimulates people to produce or consume. In deciding whether to buy something—say a house or an automobile—one can point out the objective properties of the object. One can compare alternative products, but advertisers say that unless a consumer is dazzled in his heart or titillated by his taste buds to want it, unless he really likes the house or the car, he probably will not buy it. Do not similar considerations apply to being in love? If a man loves a woman, there are no doubt objective properties that she possesses. He finds her to be beautiful; she may have a compatible personality; they may share similar values. On the other hand, a woman may be a perfect mate on a computer scale, but love may be absent because there is no *magnetism*.

MAGNETISM

We need to raise similar questions concerning fundamental beliefs, especially in regard to eupraxsophy. The quandary we face is this: Is it possible for those committed to the use of critical intelligence and scientific methods of inquiry *to arouse sufficient conviction* and *stimulate enough commitment* so that eupraxsophy can compete with the promises of religion and ideology?

We have seen the two extremes: on the one hand, unthinking faith and frenzied dogma, whether in religion or politics; and on the other hand, neutrality and skepticism, the cognitive mind-set in which a person has no strong beliefs or values, but adopts a purely reflective mode. The latter is a highly commendable approach, but it may arouse no convictions and may not be able to compete very well against powerful, antirational belief systems that promise everything.

Surely there is a middle way; surely we can develop convictions based upon the best available evidence, beliefs for which we can give reasons and which yet are of sufficient force to stimulate passionate commitment. By this I mean that at some point what at first is taken as pure hypothesis can be converted into intelligent conviction. This, I submit, is the distinctive role of eupraxsophy; that is, it expresses a cosmic outlook and a life stance, but it also arouses convictions. It appeals to both our intellect and our feelings, and it moves us to action. The eupraxsopher does not betray his objectivity in so moving, since to have passionate convictions is as essential to life as bread. Convictions cannot be disowned as alien to what we are as humans. Though philosophers may reject them as mere "persuasive definitions," the blood and guts of living require that we have some deep convictions. To have convictions is to fuse our beliefs with our attitudes, our cognitions with our feelings, our thoughts with our actions. I am using *conviction* here to refer primarily to root hypotheses or beliefs that are basic to our make-up and frame of reference, those things that we are willing to defend against attack, live and perhaps even die for, the beliefs and values we cherish most. If these beliefs are to motivate us profoundly and to hold our imagination, they must become rooted in our very being; they must give us direction, for they express our life stance. They act as a magnet upon us, drawing us back time and again to our convictions.

To say that we have convictions means that we are convinced of the truth or merits of the beliefs and values we cherish *and* that they are based on evidence, reason, or proof. To be convinced of something means that we give assent because of arguments in its favor. Doubt recedes into the background. We are willing to affirm our beliefs. We are impressed by the logic and persuaded by the evidence. We find the justification conclusive, the proof telling, the facts unmistakable. Thus the beliefs that pass these tests have enduring strength within our belief-structure, and they become convictions. But to be convinced means more than purely intellectual assent—though at a minimum it must mean that it involves emotive magnetism as well.

Every person has a large number of beliefs that he asserts as being more or less true as part of the body of knowledge. He may feel indifferent about many or most of these beliefs in the sense that he would not care if the opposite were the case. I say that the Amazon River cuts across Brazil, that Iraq has large oil deposits which it is rapidly depleting, or that there is no evidence of intelligent life on Mars or Venus. I may be convinced of the probabilities of these truth claims, but none may have much urgency for me unless I live in Brazil, Iraq, or am involved in space research. I may believe that they are true because of evidential grounds, but they are not *convictions* because convictions involve a moral dimension and an affective force. My convictions point to the basic beliefs and principles within my belief system: my cosmic outlook, my method of inquiry, my life stance, and the social polity to which I am committed. A conviction is a deep belief within my eupraxsophy.

To say that someone is a person of conviction means that he or she is truly committed to beliefs and ideals and that these operate with compelling force. A scientist qua scientist has no convictions per se, only hypotheses and theories, which he can dispense with as the evidence dictates. A philosopher qua philosopher has no convictions, only intellectual concepts, postulates, and presuppositions that are amenable to critical argument. Both the scientist and the philosopher are human beings and as such surely have their convictions, but not within their disciplines—except possibly in the decision to adopt their professions as a life stance and to use certain objective methods of inquiry. The religionist, on the contrary, has more than convictions; he has a creed and a faith, and for him, evidence or reasons recede into the background. What is vital to him is the passionate devotion and psychological need which the faith-state satisfies, often in spite of evidence to the contrary. The eupraxsopher, on the other hand, has convictions, and these are double-edged: cognitive beliefs based on evidence rationally coherent and tested by their consequences *and* attitudinal dispositions that move him to action. Convictions have cognitive form, but they also express emotive content and imperative force.

By this I do not mean to imply that a person can never change his convictions, particularly if he is committed to scientific methods of inquiry. Presumably the principle of fallibilism applies, and he may need to revise his views, however difficult this may be. Beliefs are hypothetical, and the probabilities of their truth are a function of the grounds by which they are supported. Thus we are not *bound* (*religare*) to them, because they grow out of intelligent processes of critical analysis and verification. They are reflectively grounded, but they are not simply items of intellectual assent. For once our cognitive hypotheses are transformed into convictions, they have emotional and motivational power. They are magnetic and have persuasive force.

Thus one can believe, for example, in democracy as the best form of government, and one's whole being will be prepared to die for it if it is threatened; or one can believe in the integrity of science or the importance of human rights. All of these express our convictions as humanists. But they will be empty beliefs unless they are acted upon. Thus we see that closely related to convictions are the commitments that flow from them; once we are persuaded of the truth of our beliefs and of the worth of our values, we are motivated to do what we can to implement and defend them and even to try to convince others of their truth. We are prepared to dedicate our time, efforts, and honor to see that they are implemented. We are ready to act upon them, to put them into praxis. In other words, our *sophic* convictions have a *eupraxic* role; they directly affect our conduct. Convictions are not simply internalized belief-states; insofar as they lead to commitments they spill out into the practical world in concrete terms; they guide and direct our choices and our behavior, for they express our deepest beliefs.

INSPIRATION AND ASPIRATION

Can a humanist eupraxsophy sufficiently inspire human beings to develop lofty aspirations? Religionists seize the imagination by denying human finitude, thereby overcoming the fear of mortality. They postulate unseen forces, which allegedly control our destiny and offer us salvation. Religious myths soothe the aching soul and provide an uplift. Can eupraxsophy do the same?

Millions of secularists and atheists have found life ennobling, overflowing with manifold opportunities and excitement. If a person cannot find a divine purpose to human existence, he or she can face the world with courage, accept his or her own finitude, and endure. It is not the "courage to be" that we must develop as much as the "courage to become." We are responsible for our destiny. The meaning of life is not located in some hidden crevice in the womb of nature but is created by free persons, who are aware that they are responsible for their own futures and have the courage to take this project into their own hands.

The choices that are made in life depend upon the sociocultural context in which we live, and there is a wide constellation of forces at work, including chance and luck. We were cast into the world by our parents without our consent. At some point, as we mature in life, we realize that we are responsible for our choices. Perhaps only in terms of tragedy and profound soul-searching do we raise the questions: Why am I here? What does it mean? How shall I live?

The reply of the theist is untrustworthy, for he offers spurious fairy tales spun out in the infancy of the race and has perpetuated them in continued self-deception. An objective mind cannot easily swallow the myths. But where shall skeptics turn for meaning? It is here that humanist eupraxsophy has something to say. For humanism is an effort to plumb the depths of existence, using science and philosophy, and to commit us to a life stance.

To the question "What do I want?" the humanist replies, "Why not happiness and the full life?"

To "How can I face death?" he answers, "Why not with resolute courage?"

And to "How shall I live fully?" he responds, "By sharing the creative joys and sorrows of life with others."

The tools of the eupraxsopher are not dogma or creed preached to credulous souls, but critical intelligence; not fiction, but truth. Are the responses given to a person in existential despair sufficiently eloquent so that he can be sustained in times of adversity? Can they raise the levels of aspiration to exalted heights? Can they evoke within us strenuous endeavor? Can they motivate us to achieve excellence? Do they have sufficient grandeur?

I respond: They can if they are based on *conviction* and if they can arouse *commitment* and if they call forth our *creative impulses*. Can the nonbeliever live intensely? Can he affirm his life with vigor? I do not see why not. Indeed, the pagan civilizations of the past and the humanist civilizations of the present have done so with vitality and gusto. It is possible to live exuberantly once we shed the illusions that bind us, once we overcome the corroding sense of guilt, once we enter into the world as thinking but passionate beings. Can we overcome pathological belief systems that seek to cripple us? Can we release our natural tendencies to live for ourselves and others in *this* life without the vain hope of immortality? Can we express the highest ideals? Can we affirm them in the act of living? Can we adopt a Promethean stance, shatter the gods and goddesses of the past, yet live fully as creative beings? Can we share our joys with others and have robust personal lives rich with meaning? Can we create our own plans and projects, and in fulfilling them find them intrinsically rewarding?

These are the questions that the eupraxsopher who has finally given up religion needs to consider and respond to. In the last analysis, the authentic resonance of humanist eupraxsophy is its ability not only to explain the world in the light of the best scientific evidence but also to stimulate within us passionate intensity and the will-to-live, the courage to dream of new goals and to bring them to fruition. The ultimate test of eupraxsophy is whether it helps us to lead joyous full lives and to embark upon new adventures in living.

AN INSPIRING MESSAGE

Can secular humanism provide a message that is of sufficient drama and conviction to inspire men and women to seek new heights of achievement? Can it provide ideals of such intensity and strength that it can replace the ancient myths? In each period in human civilization people must ask these questions anew in their own terms. What might be an inspiring message for the future—for the twenty-first century and beyond? No one can predict the future with certainty. No one can foretell precisely what problems and opportunities await future generations. Barring some global disaster, however, the tendencies and trends, the ideals and aspirations discernible in the present will undoubtedly continue to influence the future. No doubt people will continue to find enrichment in pursuing their careers and in relating to others—friends, lovers, members of the family, and their communities. Nonetheless, I submit that there are great humanist ideals over and beyond those which can inspire us.

We have seen how secular Marxism offered an inspiring message for the nineteenth and twentieth centuries. It broke with orthodox religion and has had an enormous appeal to millions of people, sweeping large portions of the globe. Yet Marxism suffered the same fate as many other youthful idealisms; it was corrupted by bureaucracy. Implicit also in Marxism were the seeds of its own destruction; for in its enthusiasm for a new utopia, it suppressed human freedom and was overtaken by cruelty and boredom. Although at first the defender of progress, it became the opponent of progress. Marxism proposed a more perfect society on earth, but when Marxists began to live in what they had created, it turned out to be vulgar and banal, not at all inspiring, and so its dreams became tarnished and faded.

What was essential to both Christianity and Marxism were the visions of the future that they initially promised. Both systems offered utopias: Christianity, an escape from this world to the next by means of salvation; and Marxism, an end to human injustice by the creation of a classless society. Both provided meaning for life and a glimmer of a splendid new future. Both projected images that were able to inspire countless millions of people.

Both Marxism and Christianity responded to powerful psychological forces at work deep within the human psyche. They both recognized the problem of alienation from the world, seen either as a place of existential tragedy by the Christian or by the Marxist as a corrupt economic system that denied human equality and creativity. Both have harbored resentment against those who conducted the affairs of the world. The Christian indicted the secularist for being sinful and wicked, and he focused on otherworldly dreams. The Marxist condemned the existing social system as corrupt and the ruling classes as evil, and he wished to transcend them in the future. Both were movements of ordinary people that originally appealed to the underdog: the poor, the bereaved, the oppressed, the sick, the handicapped. Both promised to redeem them. Both started as enemies of the rich and powerful, though once they seized power they created their own power structure and a new elite to replace the old.

Both systems were messianic, salvationist, and radical in their promises. Both wished to transcend the status quo by creating a new reality. It was this new reality that inspired their devoted followers and for which they would gladly sacrifice everything.

The problem with Christianity and Marxism, if interpreted as dogmatic creeds, is that they are predicated on false premises. Yet they are still so powerful that it is premature to predict their demise. Both have strong staying power and may be able to regenerate themselves. This has surely been the case with Christianity, which has survived every prognosis that it was moribund, and it may be true of Marxism, for its full history is still to be written.

Can a humanist eupraxsophy inspire men and women by the power of its images of the future? Human beings do not live by bread alone, and a viable vision of tomorrow can nourish their hopes. If humanism is to develop convictions and commitments, then its dreams must be inspiring. But how can a realistic and skeptical appraisal of the human condition have enough force to satisfy the ontic hunger of human beings for ideal meaning? Is humanism condemned to be a movement of a small intellectual elite, unable to speak to the passionate strivings of common people?

What new directions can be taken by humanism if it is to have widespread appeal? Let me suggest some possible thrilling potentialities for a better tomorrow.

Exciting New Discoveries. The scientific revolution will undoubtedly continue to afford great excitement for the human species. The frontiers of scientific knowledge are still expanding, and we do not see their end. Scientific discoveries can provide bountiful opportunities for us to probe the secrets of nature and to extend our horizons of understanding. This can lead to new technological inventions even more wondrous in their application, new products of inestimable value.

The two great sources of human enrichment are (1) increased knowledge and learning, and (2) daring new inventions and applications that can be used and enjoyed. The first must be supported by governments, universities, and research institutes, the second by industry and the economy. The discoveries of the last hundred years were deemed breathtaking in their day: the incandescent light bulb, the phonograph, the telephone, movies, television, high-speed trains, automobiles, airplanes, spacecraft, and computers. New products and services as yet undreamed of no doubt will be developed to improve and enhance life enormously.

Higher Standards of Living. All of this can contribute to the amelioration and enrichment of the conditions of human existence on a worldwide basis. It can lead to the end of poverty, a vast increase in comfort and affluence. Already large sections of the world's population are able to enjoy better lives. This can be extended to the rest of humanity if we are able to limit excessive population growth through wise family planning, so that the economic gains in agricultural production and economic development are not endangered by runaway populations. We also need to prevent unwise technologies that pollute the natural environment.

Increased Longevity. With improved nutrition and health care, it may be possible for medical science to extend human life far beyond the present limits. Medicine has already learned how to reduce pain and suffering, and to ward off premature death. But it may be possible to do so on a far greater scale, adding many years and even decades to life. Living longer, qualitatively healthier lives, the benefits to happiness can be expanded. People will be able to prolong the enjoyment of careers, friends, lovers, and families. Suffering due to premature and painful death, which much of traditional religion sought to ameliorate, suffering that was truly horrible, especially for the ordinary peasant or worker, can thus be alleviated. The conditions of life here and now can become truly bountiful and enjoyable.

More Leisure Time. The fruits of the scientific and technological revolutions have already lessened the sheer drudgery of much physical labor; and it has enabled people to have more free time to pursue activities they find rewarding. It can continue to enable them to find the means for creative occupations and pursuits, thus contributing to more rewarding lives. This includes the opportunities to enjoy the arts, travel, sports, and other forms of recreation. No one need be bored.

A Humanized Workplace. Creativity needs to be extended to the workplace. Labor-saving devices in the factory, the office, the fields, and even at home have reduced the need for toilsome labor. Clean and modern workplaces can contribute to more satisfying work. The dreadful factories of the industrial age and hard labor in the fields can give way to beautiful and more efficient methods of work. Work and play can thus be integrated as people are challenged to find their work creative. Included in this is the need to enlist people by participatory involvement in their workplace. There should be a chance for individuals to change careers in midstream, to be reeducated for new occupations; no one need be condemned to be a coal miner or a farmhand all his life, but he should be allowed to pursue other occupations at different stages in life.

Democratization and Freedom. Safeguarding individuals' rights against oppressive societies or authoritarian regimes is a challenge for the future. People should be able to live in peace and harmony without fear or cruelty. Racial, religious, and class conflict can be overcome. All human beings can be given an opportunity to participate in the institutions of their societies. Extending the ideals of the open, pluralistic, and democratic society to all regions of the globe holds forth great promise. Societies will continue to need to be regulated by laws, but these should be the products of democratic decision-making and should be open to public revision. The goal of democratic societies is to maximize the opportunities for individual autonomy and freedom of choice.

Sexual Freedom and Enjoyment. Without doctrines of repression fed by a theological erotic-phobia, human beings can learn to better appreciate and love each other; they can engage in rewarding sexual relations with other consenting adults. Responsible sexuality will enable the bonds of intimacy to develop. Women and men will be seen to be equal in dignity and worth. Couples who have reproductive freedom can practice responsible birth control and family planning. Sex does not exist solely for procreation but for recreation. Such fulfilling human relationships can contribute immensely to personal well-being.

Global Ethics in a Global Community. Human beings can come to recognize that insofar as we are all part of the world community, common human needs and rights should be respected. National, racial, religious, and political boundaries must break down, as all sectors of humanity participate in a new world civilization. This will be the sociopolitical frontier for the next few centuries, and it will need to enlist the idealism of youth and the dedication of everyone interested in building a peaceful and prosperous global community. Much hard work must be expended to fulfill this planetary vision. Also involved is the recognition that we share the same planet with other species, and that we have a duty to preserve the natural environment. Implicit in this is the obligation to seek to solve economic, social, and political problems cooperatively as integral parts of a world community.

Space Exploration. The world of tomorrow may very well open up to humankind the entire solar system and beyond for exploration. We have already entered the world of space and can leave our solar system to probe the outermost reaches of the cosmos. It may be possible to build space colonies, inhabit other planetary bodies, perhaps even voyage beyond our solar system in daring new adventures. Thus space travel can become a reality, as the planetary civilization is able to extend its reach. Viewing the earth from outer space as an interdependent global community can only inspire us to make this a reality.

Creativity. The higher forms of creativity find expression in the arts and sciences, philosophy, poetry, and music. New creative discoveries can lead to exciting and interesting experiences to be enjoyed for their own sake. Living is not simply coping with problems of survival, but it also involves creative fulfillment and actualization, the untapping of new dimensions of experience. Extending the horizons of creative learning can thus contribute to continued vitality and enjoyment.

New Horizons Yet Untapped. The prophets of doom and gloom are always predicting Armageddon. They are fearful of the future; they yearn to return to what they imagine was an idyllic past; they wish to block progress; they desire to be released from having to make choices. They predict calamity: God's wrath, nuclear destruction, the greenhouse effect, ecological disaster, economic collapse, or something else. No doubt human beings will always have problems to face. No one can escape from that. But these should be viewed as challenges, not obstacles. We need to face the future with a determination that, whatever problems may emerge, we will use our critical intelligence and resolve to solve them. The challenge of life is not to flee in despair from problems but to face them exultantly, always willing to take new voyages and adventures in living.

Hopefully, this vision of human potential and greatness can inspire people to approach life robustly, to work with others in creating a better world. If this does not inspire, then there is little more I can say. If a person is fearful of a world of unlimited new horizons, then he is perhaps beyond any reassurances that I can give. But to those who are willing to explore uncharted waters, I can only say, "Come with me to the next shore, for there are still untapped potentialities awaiting discovery. Let us affirm exultantly that life can be even more beautiful, bountiful, and wonderful."

There are radically opposed attitudes here. The contrasts are manifold: between Buddha (the contemplative soul) and Marx (the activistic stance); Muhammad (obedience to God) and John Dewey (resolving the problems of life by intelligence); Jesus (passive sacrifice to the Father image) and Prometheus (creative audacity in challenging the gods). Can the eupraxsophic Promethean stance motivate us to climb to new heights of achievement? Can it apply to every man and woman on the planet? If it is to succeed, it can only do so if we shed the fantasies of theism and move on to higher levels of attainment. There are, I submit, concrete measures to be taken. If humanist eupraxsophy is to take us in new directions, what are the next steps? These are the questions to which we must now turn.

V. Building Humanism in the Future

THE NEED FOR NEW INSTITUTIONS

One must first ask: Why have freethought, atheism, and secular humanism thus far failed to gain mass support on the world scene? Why do scientific humanists and secularists win all the intellectual campaigns against religionists, yet lose in the long run? Why do orthodox religions persist in spite of the fact that they have been dealt telling refutations by their critics? Is it because these religions are able to respond to enduring needs in the human species in a way that naturalistic humanism has not?

We are confronted with a paradox, because the forces of humanism and secularism flow very deep in civilization; indeed they are probably the strongest influence in the modern world—even synonymous with the term *modernism*. This is the Promethean resolve to challenge the gods and to understand and control nature for our own purposes. Religious institutions continue to resist the modern impulse; they do not show any signs of early demise. Though they may wane in one generation, they are apparently able to restore themselves in the next. Yet organized humanism thus far has failed in its endeavor to seize the public's imagination and to establish strong institutions as an alternative to religion.

If we were to survey the role of humanist and secularist ideas in the world today, we would be impressed by their profound impact. To mention only six: First is the development of science and the progressive application of scientific methods to the understanding of nature and life.

Second is the application of technology and industry for the betterment of the human condition, and their contributions to improved standards of living and health.

Third is the development of secular schools and universities and the extension of the horizons of learning to millions of inhabitants of this planet.

Fourth is the continued secularization of society and culture, the arts and sciences, philosophy and politics, making them independent of religious authority or control.

Fifth is the progressive development of democratic ideals worldwide, those that recognize freedom of conscience, the right of dissent, and the separation of church and state.

Sixth is the growing respect for human rights on a global scale and the sense that we are all part of an interdependent world community.

Although secularism and humanism (with a small *h* and *s*) are powerful streams in the modern world and will continue to support inspiring ideals, Secular Humanism (with a capital *S* and *H*) still has failed to gain sufficient momentum. It is true that there are some countries (particularly in Western Europe) in which the humanist movement is now growing, but the overall impact is still very weak. Some people ask: What difference does it make? As long as humanism and secularism grow, why bother to build humanist organizations per se? Humanists are independent persons and nonjoiners, they claim, and as such need no organizations to sustain them. If they no longer belong to a church denomination, why substitute membership in another institution?

I reject these arguments as rationalizations for failure. We have reached an important juncture in the evolution of human civilization, and unless strong humanist institutions are developed, there is no guarantee that the secular and humanist revolution in the modern world will continue. Secularist and humanist culture in pagan Hellenic civilization was overwhelmed by the Dark Age of Christianity; the Alexandrian Library, a treasury of great classics, was burned; and the infamous Holy Inquisition was eventually launched. Each age is in danger of new inquisitions in the name of God. There is no assurance that this will not happen again and that men and women will not retreat in fear and trembling into the false security of a religious cocoon. This might be the case if nuclear war, environmental degradation, or the population explosion were to confront humankind with problems so awesome that it feels incapable of solving them by the use of intelligence. A collapse of courage and a renewed dread of death, whether individually or collectively, can again overtake human consciousness and it may again feel the need to postulate myths of solace to ease frustration and sorrow.

If secular humanism is to be a strong power in the world and to grow, it must not be a purely cognitive affair; it must build viable social institutions to preserve the progressive gains in knowledge and to ensure that they develop in the future.

It was Karl Marx who observed that utopian socialism would remain ideal and visionary unless it used revolutionary means to apply it to *praxis*. And it was Lenin who advocated a strategy of revolution, including seizure of state power, in order to achieve results. Although I differ profoundly with Marx and Lenin—and especially disagree with their efforts to use force, violence, and state powers on society—I do agree on one point. The only way to see to it that humanist philosophical, scientific, and ethical concepts survive our age is by transforming them into conviction and commitment in the minds and hearts of ordinary men and women and by embodying them in institutional form; that is, it is by building viable institutions that secular humanism will best endure and its ideals be transformed into reality. Ideas take on a new vitality when they are reinforced by their institutional forms—though I should add, only a nonviolent strategy can most effectively accomplish this, one based primarily on moral suasion and education. Each generation should modify the ideals of the past and retain only those that are relevant to its present.

We surely do not wish to hold future generations hostage to our conceptions; yet if these ideals are viable they can help channel the behavior of ourselves and our descendants in constructive ways, without having each generation rediscover the truths we have already learned or repeat the mistakes of the past. If we fail to create new secular institutions, humanism may not have an enduring impact on civilization, especially since it has to contend daily with the residue of religious institutions of the past. In many neighborhoods it seems as though every other block has a church, temple, or mosque, and though one generation may be indifferent to their messages, the next may breathe new life into what otherwise might have been moribund shells. Sunday school classes, seminaries, sermons, revivals, and publications continue to pour forth the outdated messages of yesteryear, and a large committed clergy depend on these for their livelihood. Memories are short. Every generation must learn anew why the skeptics of the past have rejected the old-time gospels and how they have undertaken new forms of creative living. Institutions preserve the beliefs of the past and perpetuate memories of them in the future. If nothing else, the task of humanism is to build counter-institutions as alternatives to theism, else repressive forms of religiosity will continue to plague us.

Which institutions should we seek to develop? How shall we proceed in building them?

Let me point out that the modern world has already built many powerful secular institutions. For example, the modern secular state is neutral in the religious sphere, and it does not seek to enforce religious doctrines among the populace. Most

Western democracies have already wrested control of political life from theocratic powers. Similarly, the church does not exert monopolistic control over economic life, and economic institutions flourish as purely secularist phenomena. Free conscience and some measure of moral freedom are also respected independently of religion. Concomitant with the growth of secularism is the fact that democratic states now guarantee education as a universal right of all children. Parents can educate their children in secular schools, in which religious indoctrination is largely absent and the basic fund of learning, including the arts, the sciences, and a wide range of disciplines, is taught.

Viewed on the global scale, however, secularization is spotty. In many Western countries there are unremitting efforts by religionists to destroy the separation of church and state and to return religiosity to its former influence in the public square. The public schools have become a battleground, and religionists are constantly attempting to restore religiosity to them, in such forms as prayer and the teaching of "scientific" creationism. Private parochial schools exist in most Western democracies, and public funds are used to finance many of them; they compete with and weaken secular education. Moreover, there are constant efforts by religionists to impose their moral standards on the rest of society and to restrict moral freedom.

In many countries of the world the separation of church and state is still not recognized, indeed it is an incomprehensible concept. For example, in virtually the entire Muslim world nationality is interlocked with religion, and the political, economic, and moral ideology of the Koran is imposed by the state. The world of Islam has yet to experience a truly democratic revolution against theocratic control. Although Western influences are unmistakable, Islamic fundamentalists attempt to prevent the secularization of large sectors of life. Similarly, in many Latin American countries, the Roman Catholic church exerts undue authority, controlling vast wealth and exerting political power. It will no doubt be difficult to maintain the power of religion in many of these countries in the future, however, for science and technology, universal education, economic development, liberation theology, Western democratic ideals, and improved means of communication of an ever-increasing amount of information are all contesting its hegemony.

In Marxist countries the ancient churches have been shorn of much of their influence, and atheism has been proclaimed as the official ideology. Many of these countries, however, merely substituted new forms of repressive thought-control for the old, and the right of dissent has been denied. There are encouraging signs today that doctrinaire Marxism is changing and that *perestroika* (economic and political restructuring) and *glasnost* (openness) will have a positive impact on future humanistic developments in communist nations—though one cannot say with any degree of certainty what will eventuate.

In viewing the modern world, many institutions besides those of government have become secularized. It is recognized, for example, that universities and colleges can flourish only where conditions of free inquiry prevail. Hundreds of millions of young people worldwide are being exposed to the impact of higher education. Science and technology have been thoroughly secularized, as well as literature, the arts, and morality. Many institutions have been established that perpetuate secularism: art and science museums, planetariums, symphonic and other music organizations, professional societies, libraries, and the publishing houses of newspapers, magazines, journals, and books. Add to this the various forms of popular entertainment, and the secularizing influence becomes enormous. The media have a profound impact on our ideas and values, and they provide a largely nontheistic perspective. Professional sports teams, amateur games, travel and leisure activities all contribute to secularizing trends. Last but not least are the helping professions: medicine, psychiatry and counseling, hospitals and clinics—all concerned with providing health care to the sick, the helpless, the handicapped, the distraught. Although these often compete with religious hospitals and charitable organizations, they proceed on their own terms as effective alternatives to orthodox religiosity.

Where, then, is the frontier of secular humanism? It lies in building entirely new institutions that do not as yet exist. Let me suggest a creative agenda and a strategy for the future.

CRITICAL INTELLIGENCE

The primary emphasis of secular humanism has been on the cultivation of critical intelligence in society. One should not apologize for this focus, nor seek to deemphasize the centrality of cognitive thought. As I have argued, however, humanism as a eupraxsophy must seek to do more than this if it is to succeed, or else it runs the risk of being only a movement of an ineffectual, intellectual elite, with no real impact on the lives of ordinary men and women.

The first item on the humanist agenda continues to be a public education that especially develops the skills of critical intelligence, logic, and scientific methods of inquiry. We must awaken within the populace at large an appreciation of the importance of rational inquiry and thinking skills. This includes a clarification of the most effective methods for evaluating truth claims—judging them by the evidence, in light of their logical relationships, and testing them by reference to their observed consequences. Sometimes called "the hypothetico-deductive method," it is used successfully in the sciences. It involves, as I have already indicated, an open mind about questions still unresolved, and some element of skepticism about claims not objectively corroborated. It means that we should consider our beliefs to be tentative hypotheses, open to revision, until they are confirmed. Fortunately, critical intelligence is not alien to the human species; it is used in ordinary life as the mechanism by which we cope with problems of living. It is eminently practical; no one can abandon it entirely if he is to function in the real world. Everyone must remain in cognitive touch with reality and evaluate all available means in order to achieve our ends; we must also judge our beliefs by how they work out in practice. Science, I submit, is simply a more sophisticated elaboration of the ordinary modes of common sense.

Developing the skills of critical intelligence is vital in at least two senses: (1) it enables us to understand how the world in which we live and behave functions, and (2) it can help us make wise choices. The great challenge of the immediate future is to extend the methods of critical analysis from narrow specialized fields of knowledge to all aspects of thought and action, and especially to use them in appraising the claims of religion, as well as dilemmas encountered in the ethical and political domains. The task is not simply to train students in specialized disciplines for careers but to try also to get them to use their intellectual skills in other areas.

Education cannot be restricted to the schools, however. Indeed, it should be the task of all the institutions of society (economic, political, social, etc.) to help cultivate an appreciation for rational inquiry and to convey to the general public by deed as well as word the importance of such methods in furthering the quest for knowledge. The mass media have supplemented and in some ways replaced the schools as the transmission belt for information and education. It is vital, therefore, that we attempt to provide critical dissent within the media and an appreciation of alternative points of view, and that we seek to improve the quality of taste and judgment. We need to strive for excellence in newspaper and magazine articles, the publication of books, the production of films, radio, and television programs. Although the media also serve as vehicles for entertainment, producers and editors have a responsibility to keep the public well informed.

The vulgar banalities of media sensationalism should not go unchallenged.

It is clear that if citizens are to live and function in the modern world they will need to keep abreast of the increasing quantity of information. They need to appreciate the findings of science in general. Although people need to be trained for specific careers and professions, over and beyond this they need to cultivate rational powers of thought. The best therapy for nonsense is critical intelligence. Skepticism is thus an important quality of mind to cultivate in the public as an antidote to gullibility. Humanists should encourage the study of the methods of logic, of clarifying ideas, and of reaching reliable knowledge.

Education is a continuing process. It needs to address young and old alike, teaching them *how* to think and stimulating independent thought. Is it a hopeless task to seek to raise the level of intelligent debate in society? I think not. We should not denigrate the capacities of ordinary men and women for understanding and coping with difficult problems. A democracy presupposes an informed citizenry as necessary to its functioning. In any case, the primary frontier for the humanist movement is the elaboration and defense of critical inquiry in the broader society.

A CRITIQUE OF RELIGION

The methods of critical intelligence should not be viewed as intellectual skills that only a limited technocratic elite will employ in specialized fields. They can be used in all areas of life; in particular they can be employed to examine the claims of religion. The critique of religion is, however, a sensitive issue. Many humanists are reluctant to criticize the religious beliefs and practices of others within the community. "Why can't we live together in peace and harmony?" they ask. "Why not seek some kind of ecumenical understanding? If religionists will allow freethinkers the right of dissent, that is all we ask. We should avoid any attack on their religious beliefs and values." The critique of religion is considered appropriate for the village atheist, but is in bad taste in the humanist community.

Now tolerance is surely a basic humanist virtue. We do not wish to suppress the beliefs and values of those in society with whom we disagree, so long as they are not destructive of the rights of others. We need to live and let live, to respect diversity and dissent. Granted, but this surely should not guarantee everyone and anyone exemption from criticism. On the contrary, secular humanists have an obligation to submit the religious belief systems that prevail in society to intensive scrutiny. This may be dangerous, especially since criticizing another person's religious faith may be viewed as attacking that person himself. A person's identity is often defined by his religious upbringing and training. Religion may be as close to his heart as the language he speaks and the customs that he learned at his parents' knees. Religion is so intertwined with ethnicity that to hold up another person's religious beliefs or practices to criticism may be viewed by him as a threat to the very core of his being. This is regrettable, since to criticize the beliefs or practices of an individual or group need not imply any bias or hatred toward that person or group.

Do we not have a higher obligation to seek the truth and to engage other persons in constructive criticism, perhaps contributing to their self-examination and even deconversion? Why not try to persuade believers to become humanists? Most of the major religions of the world proselytize their doctrines, and they are not reticent in their criticism of competing religions. Nor are they reluctant to attack atheism, agnosticism, or humanism. For purposes of self-defense, if nothing else, humanists need to respond to the charges. The familiar litany of theism is that unbelief is wicked; those who lack religious faith are even accused of being disloyal and unpatriotic. Thus humanists need to defend themselves by examining the premises of those who would criticize them. Fundamentalists and conservatives maintain that secular humanism is a dangerous force in the modern world, and they falsely attribute immorality in the young and the breakdown of society to noxious humanist influences. Without belief in God, they moan, all is lost. Life is meaningless. Society is corrupt.

Their false indictment of humanism is made on the basis of a questionable revelatory tradition—whether it is rooted in the Bible, the Koran, the Book of Mormon, or other sacred literature. They demand adherence to the ancient faiths as the only bulwark against the influences of a suspect modernism. They are immune to the scientific method and ignorant of the higher reaches of humanist eupraxsophy.

Thus we need to ask: Is the Bible true? Should it be taken as the word of God? Does God exist? Must morality be derived from religion? Critical methods of inquiry have been applied to the sacred books of religion, particularly in the past two hundred years. These books should be read as human documents; they are not immune to critical scrutiny. When we examine them carefully we find that the claims to revelation are highly questionable, as are the moral or political imperatives that are drawn from them. In the name of God, contradictory commandments have been deduced. They have been used to condone slavery, the divine right of kings, imperialism, racism, sexism, and sexual repression, and this needs to be pointed out.

There is a strong freethought, atheistic, and rationalistic aspect of humanism which should not, in my judgment, be muted. Let us be scrupulously forthright. We find insufficient evidence for the prophets' claims of a divine revelation, a resurrected deity, heaven, hell, angels, and demons. Let us make that point without equivocation, and let us try to persuade society at large that skepticism is a responsible posture. We have examined the arguments adduced in behalf of God and we find them unconvincing. The so-called deductive proofs are fallacious, the appeals to "mystical experience" insufficient, the argument that religion is pragmatically useful questionable. The fact that some people find value in being "born again" only tells us about their psychological make-up; it does not prove the existence of a deity. *Negative criticism thus is a vital component of secular humanism, not only of the sacred cows of the prevailing religious orthodoxies but also of other irrational claims made in the public forum.* With the collapse of the ancient cults, newer paranormal and occult ones come to the fore, and these are equally deserving of critical scrutiny. We need not apologize for defending the scientific world view. We can keep an open mind about reincarnation, out-of-body experiences, immortality, precognition, levitation, psychokinesis, and UFOs, but until sufficient evidence is produced to support these claims we remain skeptical. Thus humanism and skepticism go hand in hand.

Atheism and skepticism in certain social contexts are considered extremely dangerous. True believers bitterly attack those who would debunk their dreams. The heretic, infidel, or apostate invokes intense animosity; pent-up emotional anger seeks to silence them. Fortunately, we have reached a stage in the development of human culture where dissent is tolerated. We should never return one intolerance for another; nor should we mock or ridicule alternative belief states, though we should criticize them fairly. Indeed, some sort of radical critique is essential to the lifeblood of a dynamic and creative society. This applies to exposing moral hypocrisy and political failure as well. Without a critical give-and-take in the realm of ideas, progress languishes. Regretfully, even where moral and ideological criticism is tolerated, criticism of religious ideals and institutions is not suffered lightly; it is often condemned as blasphemous. Humanism nonetheless needs to engage in constructive dialogue about the claims of religion: in the public arena, in open forums, by means of publications and books, and in the media.

ETHICAL EDUCATION

Thus far we have been dealing with the realm of ideas. But to advance the frontiers of a new eupraxsophy requires that we go beyond negative criticism and provide positive alternatives. One reason why atheism has failed is that it has been primarily destructive. It seeks to shatter the false idols which men and women worship, to expose falsity and hypocrisy; but it has not supplanted the old beliefs with positive options. It has not satisfied the hunger for imagination and poetry. Atheism has not assured society that it is prepared to sustain a responsible morality.

It is clear that humanism, if it is anything, is deeply concerned with ethics and that it cherishes moral principles and values. Often humanists have been so troubled by repressive moral codes imposed by authoritarian religions that they have sought simply to liberate society from their rigid hold. Humanism is identified with moral freedom: its program is the emancipation of the individual and society. But this is frequently believed by many defenders of the social order to contribute to the breakdown of the social fabric, that it leads to violence, crime, licentiousness, pornography, drugs, and sexually transmitted disease. Of course, it does not. But secular humanists need to spell out that although they believe in moral freedom, they wish at the same time to develop responsible ethical conduct; that they do not condone unbridled license, but believe in moderation and the rational control of desires. The differences between the two contrasting moralities is evident: (1) Transcendental theistic moral systems offer absolute commandments, and they focus on a morality of obedience to God to win salvation. (2) Humanistic ethics, on the other hand, focuses on happiness here and now and wishes to use critical intelligence to cope with problems or make moral choices.

If humanism is to have any long-range impact on society, it

must cultivate moral awareness by means of ethical education. This part of the agenda depends on the schools. What ethical principles and values should humanism seek to teach?

First is character training, the development of virtuous dispositions and the qualities of truth, honesty, dependability, loyalty, decency, and so on. Second and no less important is the cultivation of a compassionate regard for the needs of others: to be beneficent, other-regarding, empathetic; to be kind and considerate; to have good will; not to knowingly inflict harm on other persons or their property; and to be fair-minded and tolerant. The development of character does not require a belief in God: Confucius and Aristotle believed in these virtues without constructing a theology. Virtually all human communities require some moral principles; for they recognize that if we are to live together in peace and harmony, rules of civility must guide our conduct. I have called these the "common moral decencies." They are part of the heritage of humankind; they have their roots in our nature as sociobiological animals; they are a product of a long historical development within human civilization. Theists and nontheists alike share these principles. One does not have to believe in God to be empathetic or tolerant, though religions have sought to enforce some—but perhaps not all—of the moral decencies by applying divine sanctions to those who would flout them.

Humanist ethical training also wishes to develop a set of values for children, not the least of which are autonomy, independence, self-reliance, and self-control. We wish to develop responsible adults able to take control of their future destinies— not blind automata, but resourceful, creative, and intelligent human beings. Furthermore, in the modern world we seek to develop an appreciation of democratic values: shared participation in decision-making processes and toleration of differing viewpoints within the community.

Finally, any ethical education appropriate to the postmodern world will develop the skills of cognition, that is, practical wisdom. This is more than moral education or indoctrination. We wish to teach children how to deliberate reflectively, how to make wise choices and to engage in critical, rational inquiry. The field of medical ethics clearly demonstrates that age-old moral rules may not tell us what to do in many dilemmas. We may need to introduce newly elaborated ethical principles, such as informed consent and the quality of life into medical ethics, to help us make wise choices.

Ethical education presupposes that people are capable of moral growth. It does not seek to impose mere obedience to absolutes following the dicta of God. Instead it tries to develop thoughtful, considerate, decent, compassionate persons, who, following the deliberations of their moral conscience and acting as humane individuals, participate within the communities of which they are a part.

Unfortunately in many cultures morality is still considered to be the province of the religious tradition. Humanistic parents who wish to raise kind and upstanding children often have nowhere to turn. Parents who otherwise are skeptical of the claims of religion desperately feel an obligation to provide their children with moral instruction; and so they may turn to Sunday school classes in churches or temples in order to provide it.

Humanists can lead the way by developing new programs in ethical education, but ones taught from a humanistic perspective. Ethical education, of course, should have as a primary focus the family unit. By love, empathy, and constant devotion we can nurture in our children and grandchildren the art of being good, considerate, and responsible persons. Ethical education should be taught in the public schools as well; but often this kind of education is threatened by sectarian religionists, particularly in pluralistic societies where what is to be taught is open to incessant controversy. Conservatives maintain that we should teach our children reading, writing, and arithmetic. But why not the moral decencies as well? Surely, no matter what our religious affiliations, we share a common core of moral principles. Matters become open to bitter dispute when cognitive inquiry involving values clarification is introduced. Some parents fear autonomy of choice or independent thinking in their children. They wish their children to follow their guidelines and not stray from the faith of their fathers. They fear that their children may reject their views on sexual morality, abortion, or euthanasia, and that discussions with children from other racial or ethnic backgrounds could produce values at variance with theirs. The humanist replies that children have a right to know and a right to develop their own conceptions of a good life, even if their parents might disagree. Humanists should make it clear that encouraging children to think for themselves will not necessarily lead to sedition or perversion. There is a fund of collective ethical wisdom as the heritage of civilization, and children and young adults should not be deprived of the opportunity to learn these forms of cultural enrichment.

Given the realities of the political situation in some societies, where religion is still a powerful force, we need to develop alternative institutions, where ethical education, for young and old alike, can proceed. We thus come to the most distinctive new direction that humanism needs to take: to begin afresh and create an entirely new institution, one which will have as one of its vital functions ethical education.

EUPRAXSOPHY CENTERS

Let us imagine a possible scenario for the future. Let us suppose that all of the churches, temples, synagogues, mosques, and other religious places of worship in the world were to close, thereby throwing the priestly class out of work. I'm not saying that that will happen—nor even advocating that it should—though many atheists, freethinkers, and agnostics undoubtedly, have thought it a good idea for human progress. There have been periods in history when religious buildings were destroyed, as in the burning of the temple in Jerusalem in A.D. 70 by the Romans and the closing of the churches during the French and Russian revolutions; and in recent years in many Western countries churches have been closed because of low attendance.

What would be lost to society if this should happen on a world-wide scale? There would be no place where people could congregate to engage in worship and prayer, or to give vent to their sense of the divine, their reverence for sacred, unseen, and transcendent powers. Public rituals and ceremonies manifesting such piety would be unavailable, though some people might continue such practices elsewhere or in private. If the churches were closed the key rites of passage—birth, marriage, death, burial, and so on—might not be commemorated by the religious community. There might not be a traditional support system—of faith and dogmas, priests and confessors—to bolster those confronted by tragedy or overwhelmed by bereavement. The theistic response to the question "What is the meaning of life?" would no longer be available to weary souls seeking to deny their own finitude and nonbeing. Belief that God will rescue them if they engage in prescribed rituals provides consolation and helps support the priestly class. If religious organizations were to disappear, there would be no fixed solutions to moral quandaries, nor any readily identifiable moral structures to which people could turn that would tell them what was "sinful or virtuous," "good or bad," "right or wrong." Religious sanctions for the moral code might disappear. There would be no historic heritage, the faith of their fathers, to bind the members of the community together. There would be no ethnic-religious group with which they could identify.

The historic development of the house of worship played a powerful role in human culture. No doubt the idea that some ground or place, if consecrated, was thereafter sacred slowly evolved in human culture; something analogous is found in most religions of transcendence. Moreover, the idea that a cadre of professional priests would safeguard the sacred mysteries and interpret them provided this class with great power; for they held the keys to eternity and were the purveyors of the rituals that would ensure release or salvation. In classical civilizations, the pagan temples were among the most glorious architectural triumphs of the age. In medieval Europe the great cathedrals at the center of the city soared above and dominated all other edifices, expressing the majesty of God and man's devotion to him. In Muslim lands mosques were the jewels in the crown.

In many cultures rulers endowed themselves with divinity— as in Egypt, Rome, China, and Japan. The great pyramids of the pharaohs of Egypt, built to ensure them immortal life, typified the union of religious and secular power. Often an entire culture would pour forth its energies into creating grandiose monuments of magnificence, deifying human beings and honoring gods.

No longer tenable for postmodern man, these symbols of religio-political power are now seen for what they are: human creations designed to hold the common people in awe or dread of a ruling class of nobles, who used the mystery of their offices to control their subjects. Only after World War II was the Emperor of Japan shorn of his mystical, religious aura as a Living God. Veneration of political power could not have existed in the past if the subjects did not consent to obedience. Today the right of democratic self-determination rejects royal claims to power. The new symbols of the age are Promethean and democratic: skyscrapers, suspension bridges, jet airplanes, and spacecraft, the Magna Carta, constitutions, and Declarations of Human Rights. These are humanistic symbols of man's thrust to understand nature and to use this knowledge for the common good. New democratic civic virtues have replaced the ancient authoritarian symbols of earthly power.

It is likewise no longer tenable for postmodern scientific humanism to accept the symbols of the religiosity of the past, symbols that suggest there are unseen powers that control our destinies, that the divine presence is felt in places of worship, or that a self-appointed priestly class can guarantee a higher spiritual grace. That the Pope in Rome is God's representative on earth is no doubt still believed by devout Catholics, but it is impossible for anyone else to accept such a claim. We must not overstate the case; for there are liberal interpreters of religion who use metaphorical symbols, having abandoned supernaturalistic interpretations. They instead focus on an individual's inner spiritual soliloquy rather than on a communitarian interpretation of religious belief. This no doubt applies to mainstream Protestant sects, if not to orthodox Judaism, Catholicism, Islam, or Hinduism. Some liberal religionists reject the idea of supine obedience and they revolt against any authoritarian priestly class. They reject any fixed creed or doctrine. They consider it their right to select their own ministers and to fire them if they do not measure up to their standards. Yet they have many of the outward trappings of religion, including the house of worship.

Do church or temple buildings, if demystified, have a function to perform? One thinks immediately of the churches of the Unitarian Universalist Association and other liberal denominations that have a low level of dogma or ritual and have been largely demythologized. What functions do they support?

Should secular humanists create centers? Do they need buildings? Do people who reject religion entirely need to bring into being special places where they can congregate and meet? If so, what would they do there? Does this suggest that a nonreligious secular humanism would be aping religion? A strong atheist would deny any need for a center. He is so opposed to the baneful effects of dogmatic religion that he does not wish to create analogous institutions. He sees no point to prayer or ritual. There is no need for clergy. Why perpetuate the superstitions of the past? Why build secular humanist centers or edifices?

There is some merit to his argument: Let us make a clean break with religion, which was predicated on false premises; let us start afresh and take new directions. Nonetheless, some needs of human beings cry out to be satisfied. I submit that if humanist eupraxsophy is to be an effective and enduring social force, it can do so only by creating institutions that will satisfy some of these needs. To get directly to the point: There does not exist for secularists and freethinkers who have abandoned religious beliefs adequate social mechanisms to deal with a number of fairly perennial human needs. I submit that we need to establish new institutions in postmodern society that will do so. What are these needs?

The Need for *Sophia*

Science and Philosophy. There is a need for an institution in society that will provide some wisdom in life. Its first task will be to try to relate the various strands of the body of knowledge at any one time in history into some comprehensive whole. In other words, we can create Eupraxsophy Centers that will interpret what we know about nature and human life in meaningful terms. Such centers will be concerned with the frontiers of science and technology, seeking to explain their findings and to convey some sense of the creative adventure of learning. Many social and cultural institutions today attempt to make science and technology understandable to the public: the public schools and colleges and universities provide courses and curricula on various aspects of science; a great number of scientific journals and books are published each year; science museums and planetariums exhibit the world of science. Yet if science is the most daring new revolutionary force in the modern world, there can never be too much science education. Thus, the first task of Eupraxsophy Centers is to dramatize the scientific world view in popular and understandable terms to nonspecialists and the public in general.

Philosophy can be enlisted in this venture, because the

philosopher of science, working closely with scientists, is often able to translate technical scientific concepts into meaningful language. But we also can use the arts and music to dramatize what we have learned about nature. Probably the most eloquent rendering of the scientific world is found in the planetarium-museum, which uses a pictorial medium in order to depict graphically the universe that astronomy and other sciences are studying. Here what were formerly believed to be divine mysteries are translated into naturalistic causal explanations. Thus we can convey some appreciation for the scientific voyage into the unknown. Humanism is cosmic in its outlook, and science is the key to understanding the universe. Science, however, should not be presented in purely cognitive terms. Its facts can be portrayed by using all the techniques of modern literature and the arts along with science, to describe the spectacle of nature that science reveals. Music and rhythm, painting and poetry can be accompaniments to the natural order, expressing man's highest aspirations: the quest for truth and our heroic efforts to plumb the depths of being.

Critiquing Religion. Such Centers would reject religious interpretations of reality, They would do so with good reason, but they can spell out why humanists do not believe in God. Humanist eupraxsophers are committed to a naturalistic world view and to humanist ideals and values, but they need to demonstrate why theism has failed to support the god-idea and immortality of the soul. Atheist and freethought centers that make available the best literature of skepticism are virtually nonexistent on the cultural scene of most countries. What is needed are libraries of the freethought tradition, magazines, books, films, and television programs about unbelief. The contest for the minds and hearts of men and women can only be waged at first on intellectual grounds. The case against theism and for naturalistic humanism must begin with skeptical critiques.

As I have already indicated, many humanists are polite, fearful of being critical of their neighbors' beliefs, but humanism will not make any substantial headway unless it clearly states why it is areligious. In this educational mission, Secular Humanist Centers will present the best philosophical arguments of the past, by men such as Carneades, Hume, Voltaire, Diderot, Nietzsche, Freud, Marx, Russell, Sartre, Dewey, and others. Literature, novels, poetry, drama, and music are vital to this effort, but we need to go beyond this.

Applied Critical Thinking. In normative terms, Eupraxsophy Centers will need to do what they can to develop the skills of critical thinking. One cannot leave this mission to the public schools, colleges, or universities alone, important as they are. Colleges and universities have become supermarkets, where students sample a variety of courses, from English poetry to botany, from music to gymnastics. Students are usually left to themselves with little guidance. Using the elective system, they are often unable to integrate the body of knowledge to which they have been exposed. Given our pluralistic society, it is exceedingly difficult for the public schools, colleges, or universities to become instruments for education with a secular humanist outlook. These schools teach secular and humanist subjects, and they seek to cultivate competence in a wide range of fields, but they are unable to weave them together or to compete with the theistic picture of reality in society at large. Were they to do so explicitly, no doubt there would be demands that the public withdraw its financial support, and conservatives would indict the schools for teaching the "religion of secular humanism." Teaching the skills of critical thinking is permitted today, so long as it does not challenge the status quo of religion, morality, and politics. Were it to do so in a serious way, there would be howls of protest. Accordingly, a significant part of the educational mission of a Eupraxsophy Center must be to provide courses and curricular materials so that students may learn how to think and how to use objective methods in evaluating claims to knowledge. This is essential for anyone who wishes to live in the modern world and to cope with the problems that emerge. One can master a discipline and also absorb a great deal of information; but unless one can think critically about what one learns, one has no procedure for appraising truth claims in religion, morality, and politics. Thus, intensive study of the methods of inquiry are essential. This study should not be purely intellectual, of idle theoretical significance, but should also have practical significance; it needs to be applied to life itself.

Eupraxia

Meaning of Life. Eupraxsophy Centers will need to focus on eupraxia, good practice. They should deal with questions concerning the meaning of life, presupposing that the examined life is worth living. Once a person is liberated from the theistic world view and once he can use objective methods of inquiry, his next task is to find creative sources for meaningful expression. This task may very well become a central starting point for the Center. Many people are at sea, lost in a maze of misinformation, unable to make sense out of their personal fives, mired in confusion and despair. Not able to find themselves or to decide what they wish to get out of life, they flounder unmotivated and uncertain about which occupation or career they wish to enter or what they should do with their lives.

The humanist eupraxsopher has adopted a life stance. He has clarified his first principle of ethics. He is aware of what he cherishes most in life. Thus, central to the educational mission of the Center can be the theory and practice of ethics, with special focus on practice. The Center can provide an environment in which moral dilemmas can be discussed openly and honestly—euthanasia, abortion, divorce, sexual morality, war and peace, the ethics of nuclear power, male and female roles, and so on. These questions can be debated without dogma or indoctrination, using the best critical intelligence to resolve disagreements.

But the Center is more than that; it is not simply a school. It can also be a laboratory for lived experience. It can provide a setting for people to actually relate to each other.

Ethical Education. Moral education of children will be a primary function of the Center. It needs to bring the best skills of educational psychology to the learning process. It will seek to cultivate in the young habits of virtue and character, nourish compassion and empathy, encourage autonomy and responsibility, develop cognition and practical thought. This means courses, projects, and teachers with the skills required to nourish moral growth in the young. A useful adjunct to this program would be courses in ethical education for parents as well.

Counseling. The Center can also provide counseling services for all age groups: career counseling for those seeking alternative occupations and professions; drug or alcohol-abuse counseling for those who need help to overcome addiction; marriage and sex counseling for those who are in pain and difficulty; and last but not least, grief counseling for the suffering that tragedy or death brings. It should use the best professional talent available to assist in the counseling services.

Creative Renewal and Friendship. These Centers can also provide opportunities for creative renewal, not only intellectually but also emotionally. They can help to arouse conviction and commitment, to raise levels of inspiration and aspiration. One of the purposes of the Center is to provide a place where good fellowship can flourish. The Center will thus function as a support group, providing fraternal bonds of solidarity.

In a mass-oriented, media-focused society, people all too often have little opportunity to meet others. Friendship centers can serve as community centers, where a wide range of activities are sponsored: lectures, picnics, hikes, trips to museums and theaters, concerts, films, and dance. They can provide a setting for shared experiences between like-minded friends.

Rites of Passage. For many freethinkers, celebrating the rites of passage is a controversial aspect of humanism. We enjoy celebrations with family and friends at pivotal moments in life: the birth of a new child; graduation from grammar or high school, college or university; the opening of a new office; the embarking on a new job; marriage; birthdays; anniversaries; retirement. It would be appropriate for the Eupraxsophy Center to make note of these joyous moments by some kind of ceremony: a wine and cheese party, a birthday cake, the giving of presents, singing, and poetry.

Similarly, it is well for others to help us endure our sorrows: the loss of a child or a parent, a painful divorce. Commemorative ceremonies may soothe the aching heart and provide some solace in truly naturalistic terms. One is not imitating religion if one throws a party to mark a joyous event or to celebrate a marriage, or if on a special occasion one reminisces about a person who has died and remembers his or her beauty as a person.

Enjoyment. In a pluralistic, mass-oriented, and otherwise religious society, freethinkers too can share their appreciation for moral poetry. Humanist Eupraxsophy is committed to the good life here and now, to reaching joyful and exuberant happiness, and it can do no less than express this. Central to humanist eupraxsophy should be humor: comedians, humorists, laughter, fun and games—that is the fruition of life at its finest. Thus swimming parties, card games, dances, and other activities would enhance the Center, which should be a place for information and education but also for entertainment. Humanism is concerned with using intelligence to plan for the future, but it is also the *present moment of experience* that needs to be savored for its own sake. Thus the Center can contribute in a modest way to enhancing the quality of life and creative enjoyment. I am not denying, of course, that the Center has serious purposes and goals, but surely there is something more than that to life, and mirth equally needs to be encouraged.

Social Polity. Last but not least, Eupraxsophy Centers can be a place where we can discuss our concerns about the good society and social justice. This aspect is apt to be the most contentious, and one has to be careful that the Center does not develop a doctrinaire party line. Central to humanism is the appreciation for diversity and uniqueness. We are likely to differ as human beings about any number of questions; we need to appreciate the idiosyncratic eccentricities among us. We share social and political ideals—a commitment to separation of church and state, a democratic society, the defense of human rights and civil liberties. Members within the community may wish to organize separate committees to work for any number of social causes, but it would be folly for them to speak for the entire corporate Center or deny the right of dissent. The Center would not endorse political candidates or political programs save in dire emergencies when the democratic society is endangered. It should allow free room for the heretic or freethinker in politics—all in the spirit of dialogue and tolerance.

THE EUPRAXSOPHERS

Humanism believes in democracy, not only in theory but also in practice. Thus these Centers should provide an opportunity for participatory democracy. Opposed to the humanist ideal is that of orthodox religions, where a priestly class lays down the rules which parishioners or worshippers are bound to obey dutifully.

This authoritarian model is alien to the entire ethical philosophy of humanism.

A word of caution: Participatory democracy will not succeed unless there is intelligent leadership, which can help crystallize beliefs and values and provide some direction. Thus a Center needs to combine participation with some kind of effective representative leadership, someone qualified by knowledge and virtue.

I have seen existing humanist organizations languish ineffectually because their voluntary lay leaders were incompetent, not sufficiently dedicated, given to wrangling and infighting. Perhaps some of this is endemic to voluntary associations, which are prone to conflict. Surely other institutions in society also experience internal splits and battles. Thus, participants at the Center would need to develop an intelligent commitment to democracy, a sense of fair play, the spirit of cooperation, a willingness to allow different points of view, and a desire to negotiate differences after adequate dialogue and debate. Each Center should be fairly autonomous in its self-governance. It will need to blend two principles: (1) participatory democracy, in which the members of the Center have a real sense of belonging, a stake in formulating the policies and practices of the Center, and a sense of responsibility to its furtherance and well-being; (2) intelligent leadership with sufficient competence and know-how to be effective, capable of providing thoughtful guidance, able to represent the views of its members.

The only way that humanist eupraxsophy will succeed is if we establish special schools to educate leaders and counsel teachers. The best term to describe a humanist leader is *eupraxsopher*, and only when he has demonstrated that he has both wisdom and virtue, and that he is able to practice them.

Who are the ideal eupraxsophers? Men and women who have been trained cognitively in science and philosophy, who have a sense of history, who are informed about the latest frontiers of knowledge, and who are capable of ethical reflection. They should be morally decent persons with integrity, trustworthy, compassionate, and fair-minded. They should exemplify three basic virtues: character, compassion, and critical intelligence. Such individuals express the values of *excelsior*, or excellence: they have a sense of their own autonomy, are capable of making responsible choices, have self-respect, are highly motivated in outlook, and manifest good will. The eupraxsopher recognizes the importance of attaining personal happiness and exuberance in life; but he also has empathy, is responsible to the community in which he lives, and to the world community.

The eupraxsopher, then, is an ethically decent person: self-reliant, yet other-regarding; capable of self-mastery and self-control; aware of his own interests, yet able to live with and work for others in cooperative projects.

It is depressing to encounter humanists who are unpleasant people, individuals who stoutly reject religious faith and who are committed to improving the condition of humanity, yet who are personally disagreeable. This is not unique to humanists; nonhumanists can be equally obnoxious. Such personalities have dispositions like dried-up prunes; they are sour and unpleasant, even mean-spirited toward their fellow human beings. Thus, paying heed to humanist character is vital. If humanism means anything, it should lead to good manners, and it should focus on educating intelligent, creative, and resourceful people who are cheerful and exude a positive outlook on life. Some people are excessively negative or pessimistic. Nothing seems to work for them; everything turns out badly. If one has a defeatist attitude, then this can sire failure. Why not be optimistic? Since we have but one life to live, why not enjoy it now as best we can? Granted that we may encounter difficult problems, but let us attempt to ameliorate poor conditions and improve them in the future.

I should point out that humanist eupraxsophers should be capable of enjoying life. They should not be bound by debilitating sexual repression or a distorted sense of guilt. Sexual expression can be a rich and exciting source of enjoyment. The eupraxsopher should be able to balance his or her needs and wants, feelings and desires in intelligent harmony.

The eupraxsopher is the opposite of the religionist, who is full of reverence and obedience and is fixated on salvation. The eupraxsopher has a realistic sense of his own powers and limitations, and he wishes to use intelligence and effort to create a meaningful life for himself, his family and friends, and to contribute where he can to the community. The philosopher loves analytic wisdom but seems incapable of applying it to his life. The scientist knows his specialty and may know it well, but he may no more be able to lead the good life than the average shoemaker or mechanic. If humanism is to succeed, it needs to educate a vanguard of eupraxsophers who embody the best practical virtues and excellences in shared democratic communities.

Alas, we do not now have schools or colleges where eupraxsophers can be educated. Our universities have become megauniversities, and our colleges training grounds for the careers and professions. The earlier ideal of a liberal-arts education is continually eroded in the contemporary world. Hence, we need to develop thoroughly humanistic centers of learning, focusing on educating the full person, liberating him from ancient dogmas and fears, providing him with the opportunities for creative actualization and moral excellence. Perhaps some colleges and universities can be persuaded to return to this mission; until they do, we need to establish humanist schools, which will train individuals to be eupraxsopher-leaders and will educate ordinary men and women to follow the ideals of humanist eupraxsophy in word and deed.

In more practical terms, it may be difficult at first to find eupraxsophers of sufficient competence and mastery who are gifted with theoretical scientific and philosophical knowledge *and* ethical wisdom. Accordingly, we need to enlist the help of scientists to give lectures, courses, and seminars: astronomers who can convey a sense of the majesty of the cosmos; natural and biological scientists who can impart enthusiasm for the frontiers of knowledge of the biosphere; social and behavioral scientists and historians who can do the same in their fields; and ethical philosophers who are capable of providing normative insight into practical ethical choices. Similarly, we will need to enlist volunteers to participate in the cooperative efforts of the Center and to assume part of the responsibility for its success.

I have been using the term Eupraxsophy Center. Perhaps there are better terms. Some have suggested that they be called Secular Humanist Centers. Others have suggested Humanist Friendship Centers, for presumably they will be places where people can congregate on social terms. Still others have wished to call them Humanist Communities, Humanist Societies, or Humanist Groups. Perhaps none of these terms fully conveys what is intended. Let me suggest some alternatives: Humanist Eupraxsophy Centers, Creative Renewal Centers, Meaning of Life Centers. Here is one to delight: Why not call them Eupraxsotheques, meaning places (-*otheques*) where eupraxsophy goes on, like discotheques (where music is heard) and bibliotheques (in French, a place for books)?

What I have suggested is ambitious. No doubt it will require massive investments of time and capital. But, I submit, if humanism is to be fully effective, it will need to provide ambitious working models on a grand scale.

BEYOND ETHNICITY

The final issue I wish to address is perhaps the most important: Is it possible to develop a new *identity*, one that transcends the partial loyalties of ethnicity, nationality, race, or religion? An enduring trait of the religiosities of the past is that they tied a person to an ethnic heritage. One cannot easily tamper with ethnicity. Historically, the gods were tribal gods. Each clan, city, or nation had its own religion. Belief in the sacred deities was transmitted almost by osmosis to everyone living within the territorial group. The Gypsies and the Jews were able to move across frontiers, but these were close-knit, consanguineous groups where intermarriage with outsiders was frowned upon.

Religions define a person's being; but this is largely a matter of birth. I am no doubt overstating the case; for there have been periods of mass conversion and there has always been some intermarriage. Nonetheless, learning a religion is like learning a language, absorbing the cultural norms and values of the social group. The world today is divided into contending religious ethnicities; one may be an Irish Catholic, a Scots-Irish Protestant, a Norwegian Lutheran, a Sephardic Jew, a Sunni Muslim Turk, a Shia Muslim Iranian, or an Indian Hindu. One's ethnic origin gives meaning and identity to one's being. The religious beliefs of one's parents, grandparents, and great-grandparents are lovingly imparted to the children's children, and these children's memories are significant in their consciousness. Some religions today cut across national frontiers. Yet being a Roman Catholic or Jew or Protestant itself becomes essential to one's classification. Many people find their ethnic identity to be meaningful; certain qualitative values pervade a person's outlook and bonds the community into a tradition. Overall, ethnic tribal religion gives deep historical rootings for a person's beliefs and values.

There is clearly something arbitrary about all of this, for ethnicity depends upon the accident of birth, of geography and breeding. Children are indoctrinated into a religious tradition without their consent. They may be baptized at birth and confirmed at puberty, and if their parents are religious throughout their formative years, their religion is instilled gradually by training and practice. For most people, religious faith is not a matter of free conscience, although later in life some heroic dissenters may break decisively with their religion and adopt a new set of beliefs. Still, if born under a different part of the sky, most individuals would have different religions.

The close identification of religion with ethnicity has its negative features. It may pit peoples against one another; it may engender narrow-mindedness. For orthodox believers, marriage outside their religious clan is forbidden, and those who breach the prohibition may suffer punishment or exile. Where preserving ethnic identity is strictly enforced, an ethnic group may develop an apartheid psychology. There seems to be a fairly common tendency to favor members of one's own clan, tribe, race, religion, or language, and to regard those of other ethnicities and religions as strange, sacrilegious, or even immoral. This view can exacerbate hatred, conflict, and warfare. Preserving a religio-cultural tradition has somewhere the richness of cultural diversity merit in a polyethnic world is cherished, but it has its serious drawbacks insofar as one appreciates only one's own cultural heritage and not others. This prevents us from reaching common ground with other human beings. Can we transcend our narrow ethnic loyalties? Can we overcome the parochial religious traditions that divide people? The segregationist and dehumanizing tendencies of chauvinistic religion are a strong argument against them. "You must accept my creed or faith and share my ethnic heritage or you are not fully human," says the strict religionist.

Can the person who breaks with his religious background develop a *new identity that is universal rather than parochial in focus*? To the humanist, a person is a member of the human species before he is anything else. One's national, ethnic, or racial membership is derivative and cannot stand in the way of higher obligations to the whole of humankind. Humanist eupraxsophy is thus global in focus. No matter what a person's condition of birth and regardless of his or her national origin, race, class, creed, or sex, all human beings should be considered equal in dignity and value. Each person is to be regarded as precious, his or her rights are to be respected, regardless of whether we share beliefs and values. Humanism thus brings the human species to a higher plane of consciousness. Unlike the Sectarian religions of the past, humanism is the harbinger of a new universalistic eupraxsophy, in which all humans can share the same identity. We are all members of the new planetary society that is now emerging. The humanist eupraxsopher recognizes that though each of us may be born white, black, brown, or yellow, French or German, American or Japanese, male or female, each of us is a member of the human species and a part of the world community.

Humanists recognize that the isolated breeding pockets of the past have resulted in separatist ethnic divisions. Humankind is divided into different races, cultures, tribes, nations, castes, religions, and ideologies, many of which evolved before the dawn of skeptical philosophy and science and before they could be scrutinized by reason. Muslims or Sikhs, Hindus or Jews, Biafrans or Quebecois, Protestants or Catholics, Russians or Chinese are each defined by what they are geographically and genetically. Travel and communication, emigration and immigration, fraternization and intermarriage, however, have now mixed the human family to such an extent that we live in a common though polyethnic world. A realistic appraisal of the human condition on this planet is such that the narrow loyalties of the past are no longer adequate for the future.

Granted, we need to respect cultural differences, not eradicate them; we need to appreciate the manifold contributions of diverse human communities. They each have some qualities that we can appreciate and enjoy: beautiful differences in arts, language, music, cuisine. We have reached a stage, however, where a universal ideal needs to supplement the cultural worlds of the past.

There are common human rights that must be respected by everyone. We are all citizens of a new planetary community; a new global ethics is emerging. We may wish to retain those parts of our ethnic heritages that still have some value, but we need to move on to a new plateau, in which all persons can participate.

We need to learn to live together as part of the new world culture that is emerging. The challenge is to develop a *new identity* that matches this culture, that focuses on our common interrelated outlook and values.

Although we are still divided by language and culture, religion and ideology, nationality and ethnicity, the world of the future can truly become a humanist world, a world in which contentious ethnic differences are transcended. But if this is to occur, then we need to develop radically new ways of thinking and feeling.

Humanist eupraxsophers are convinced that humanism affords humankind ideals that are eminently practical and truly inspiring. They believe that humanism can help us reach new heights of excellence. Humanism can produce progress without the delusional systems of the past. We are capable of enjoying the world of the present, but we must be prepared to embark upon the adventures of living in the world of tomorrow. Whether a humanistic world will ever come into being depends upon our efforts and resolve, and upon whether we can break finally with the ancient religions of the past, move beyond them, and build a truly humane world in the future.